The New
TERRORISM

To Martha

SINE QUA NON

CONTENTS

1.

TERROR WEARS MANY MASKS

Kidnapping. Assassination. Skyjacking. Hostage-taking. Bombing. Armed robbery.

An apartment in Verona, Italy. A parade ground in Cairo, Egypt. An abandoned airfield near Amman, Jordan. The U.S. embassy in Teheran, Iran. A street in Paris, France. A suburban shopping mall in Nanuet, New York.

Such are the six most typical operations favored by today's terrorists. Such are the far-flung locations in which they are carried out.

1. The Kidnappers

General James L. Dozier answered the knock on his apartment door. Two men in work clothes were waiting outside. One of them muttered something in Italian. Dozier couldn't quite catch what the man said. He remembered that his wife had sent for the plumbers. He led them to the leaky kitchen sink.

Something steel-hard crashed into the side of Dozier's

1

head. He went down. Grabbing at the men's legs, he tried to claw his way back up. More gun-butt blows rained down. Dozier caught a quick sideways glimpse of his wife, forced to her knees, a pistol pressed to her head. He quit struggling.

Two more intruders strode in, dragging a steamer trunk. They blindfolded Dozier and gagged him. Then they manhandled him into the trunk and banged the lid tight.

During the next hour Dozier came close to fainting several times for lack of air. He was aware of being transported in some kind of vehicle. When the vehicle stopped and the trunk was hauled out, it suddenly seemed to swing free as if being hoisted high in the air. Finally it came to rest.

Released at last from his coffinlike confinement, the still blindfolded Dozier could feel the men handcuffing his right wrist to something, and then his left ankle. They yanked the blindfold off.

He was seated on a cot inside a tiny blue tent. Through the tent's one open end he could see that it had been set up inside some sort of room, but few details were visible in the dim light. Obviously they meant to make sure he'd never be able to identify the place.

The date was December 17, 1981. Dozier was to spend forty-two grim days fettered to that cot. He could barely stretch his legs or move around. For a man accustomed to jogging three miles a day, being deprived of physical exercise was a real agony.

He knew almost at once that his captors could only be a part of Italy's dreaded Red Brigades. These heavily armed ultra-radical terrorists had disrupted Italian so-

ciety for nearly a decade. Three years earlier they had
shocked the world by kidnapping Aldo Moro, a former
prime minister of Italy. After fifty-five days, during
which thousands of policemen and soldiers had virtually
ransacked the country, Moro's bullet-riddled body was
found in the back of a car on a side street in Rome.

The jittery nation had barely recovered from the
Moro trauma. It was only the worst of hundreds of Red
Brigade kidnap-murders that scarred the 1970s. Democracy, still a relatively new way of life in Italy, was in
grave danger. The Red Brigades' goal of revolution
seemed perilously close.

General Dozier was the first American they had ever
snatched. His job as deputy chief of staff for NATO
forces in southern Europe made him an especially valuable prize. The terrorists tried to interrogate him several times, probing for NATO military secrets. The
tough West Pointer and Vietnam combat veteran gave
them nothing usable.

Dozier noted that after a few days they stopped
bothering to wear hoods or to blindfold him. Apparently they no longer felt there was any reason to hide
their identity. Only one explanation seemed possible:
like Moro, he'd been sentenced to death.

Meanwhile, the terrorists issued periodic statements
to the press. Dozier was denounced as "the hangman of
NATO." A photo was published of Dozier posed in
front of a Red Brigade banner. He could be seen holding a placard emblazoned with "anti-imperialist" slogans. His unshaven face still bore the bruises he'd received on the day he was kidnapped.

Though Dozier knew nothing about it, the biggest

manhunt in Italy's history was under way. As the days dragged by, the police efforts began to pay off. Key Red Brigade suspects were picked up, and some began to talk.

On January 28, 1982, in an operation timed with split-second precision, a detachment of Italy's specially trained anti-terrorist experts, the so-called "Leatherheads," burst into the hiding place. One of the kidnappers desperately pointed a pistol at Dozier, but the Leatherheads instantly clubbed the gunman to the ground. The rescuers brought the happily grinning general out into the sunlight.

For the Red Brigades, as we shall see, it was the beginning of near-total catastrophe.

2.   The Assassins

Anwar Sadat, president of Egypt and supreme commander of its armed forces, was not his usual energetic self that morning. His vice-president urged him to stay home and rest. But this was a proud occasion, and Sadat would not miss it. It was the anniversary of the great victory of October 6, 1973. Eight years ago he had sent Egypt's armies storming across the Suez Canal, taking the Israelis by surprise.

A full-scale parade was planned. Troops and tanks and guns would stream past the presidential reviewing stand for several hours, while jets thundered overhead. Sadat was resplendent in a specially tailored new uniform, its dark blue glittering with gold braid and ornamented with a star-encrusted green sash. Promptly at

10:00 A.M. he took his place of honor between the vice-president and the minister of defense. The march began.

Every conceivable security measure had been taken to protect the president and the hundreds of distinguished guests around him in the reviewing stand. Above all, the security men had checked every weapon included in the parade. Carrying live ammunition was strictly forbidden.

By 12:40 P.M. the parade was about half over. Six Mirage jets zoomed low over the crowd; all eyes followed them. At that precise moment one of the trucks in the parade halted directly in front of the presidential box. Hardly anyone noticed the three uniformed men in the back of the truck as they leveled their automatic rifles.

A deadly spray of lead and steel raked the reviewing stand. A fourth assassin broke out of the truck's cab, hurled a grenade into the crowd, and opened fire as he moved in. The others also raced toward the stand, firing all the way.

The crowd in the reviewing stand exploded into turmoil. Almost everyone in the first few rows went down; it was hard to tell how many had actually been hit. The lucky ones who had escaped injury cringed among the bleeding bodies of the dead and wounded. Hundreds of others scrambled desperately for safety in every direction. The air resounded with screams, sobs, curses.

No one had made a move against the terrorists. Two of them now raised their guns high over their heads, triggering streams of slugs directly downward into the front-row-center area where Sadat had fallen. The body of the already unconscious president twitched helplessly as the bullets thudded into him.

At last the security men reacted. Automatic rifles bucking in their hands as they returned fire, they charged after the killers. One assassin screamed and fell, badly wounded. Three others, their ammunition used up, threw down their guns and surrendered.

They had accomplished their mission. Anwar Sadat—the man of peace, the only Arab leader who had dared make peace with Israel—was dead.

His killers were members of a fanatical Muslim sect, *Jamaat al Taqfir wal Hijra* (Society for Repentance and Retreat). Its members were spread throughout the country and were active in a wide range of professions. Some occupied influential, strategically sensitive positions in the police and the military services.

These men, mostly in their middle twenties and early thirties, bitterly opposed Sadat's efforts to modernize and reform Egypt. They insisted that Egypt must return to the strictest and most orthodox form of Islamic faith, restoring all laws and customs hallowed by tradition. Never could these passionately devout Muslims accept the new relationship with Israel.

If they had hoped that their bloody act would unleash a revolutionary overthrow of the government, they were doomed to disappointment. The vice-president simply replaced the dead president, as the constitution prescribed. The nation moved forward.

Six months later, having been duly convicted by a military court, the killers were executed.

3. The Skyjackers

The empty and abandoned airfield baked soundlessly in the desert sun. No planes had landed or taken off here in years. The field lay forty miles from the nearest city, Amman, capital of Jordan. A newer airport had been built closer to the city.

Slowly mounting in volume, the whine of an approaching jet pierced the air. As the plane came in and landed, the TWA logo was clearly visible on the huge Boeing 707. Within hours, it was joined by a Swissair DC-8 and a British Viscount 10. No passengers emerged from any of them.

Several hundred miles away, another jumbo jet landed at the airport in Cairo, Egypt. It bore the markings of Pan Am. Again, no one came out.

The date was September 6, 1970. The biggest, most sensational skyjacking operation in history was under way.

Masterminding the entire complex operation was a Palestinian physician named Waddih Haddad. With his longtime colleague, Dr. George Habash, he had led a group of angry young Palestinians in the late 1960s to form the extremist Popular Front for the Liberation of Palestine (PFLP). With its total dedication to the violent destruction of Israel, the PFLP was one of the more radical groups operating within the broad framework of the Palestine Liberation Organization.

This quadruple skyjacking was the PFLP's latest effort to force concessions out of the Israelis. The skyjackers demanded that Palestinians in Israeli prisons be released and flown to friendly countries. Israel was to yield territories captured from the Arabs in the 1967 war.

The PFLP had at first directed its hijack operations exclusively against Israel's El Al airline. Starting in 1968, several El Al jets had been forced to destinations in countries friendly to the Palestinians' cause.

The Israelis had countered with armed guards on all flights. Locked, bulletproof doors now blocked access to the flight decks in all El Al airliners. In one PFLP attempt to hijack an El Al plane, the guards had killed one hijacker and captured the Palestinians' most famous female activist, Leila Khaled.

Now Haddad and his followers had decided to test the Western powers' influence over the Israelis. Perhaps a multiple skyjacking, directed not against El Al but against American and British aircraft, with several hundred mostly Western passengers held hostage, would achieve a breakthrough.

The four planes, three American and one British, sat ominously still beneath the merciless sun. At length, contact was established between the hijackers and the authorities. PFLP spokesmen stated their demands. The hijackers warned that they were already placing explosive charges at strategic points in the four big jets. Refusal would lead to destruction of the planes, the passengers, and even, if necessary, the terrorists themselves.

The negotiators conveyed the demands to the Israelis swiftly, but not very optimistically. Israel's experience with terrorism was long and bitter. By 1970 Israeli policy had hardened into clear and uncompromising terms: no negotiations and no concessions whatsoever.

The Israelis were firmly convinced that giving in led only to more attacks and constantly escalating demands.

For hours, eventually stretching into days, the negotiations dragged on. In the end, the hijackers were persuaded to release all the passengers and crew members in exchange for safe conduct to selected destinations for themselves.

But the planes were not released. They were the terrorists' last desperate card, and they would play it. The preset explosive charges needed only the closing of a few electrical contacts. In full view of television cameras transmitting the incredible scene instantly to millions of viewers around the world, the four silver craft, valued at over $20 million each, disintegrated in four separate, simultaneous eruptions.

4. The Hostage-Takers

Marine Sergeant James M. Lopez could hear the mob approaching the U.S. embassy compound. Here in Teheran, the capital of Iran, that sound had become all too familiar lately.

Lopez was none too delighted about being the only guard on duty that Sunday morning. Was this going to be just one more anti-American demonstration, or might things get more serious this time? He'd have to move fast to prevent any real trouble.

The demonstrators straggled into sight. As usual they carried a ragtag assortment of slogans, signs, and banners. Some read "Death to Amerika." Others read "Give us the shah." Many marchers carried big blown-up photographs of their revolutionary leader, Ayatollah Ruhollah Khomeini.

An ayatollah is a high official of the Muslim faith. The Ayatollah Khomeini was chieftain of the militant Shiite sect, which preaches a return to basic Islamic principles. It was in Khomeini's name that the Iranian people had overthrown the shah and driven him into exile earlier in 1979.

The once mighty shah, seriously ill with cancer, had been admitted to the United States for medical treatment. Khomeini was outraged. He and his followers angrily demanded that the United States return the shah to Iran for trial as a traitor and criminal.

Now Lopez stood alone, facing the angry mob. He checked his weapons. He noted with relief that a good supply of teargas grenades was at hand. A few whiffs of the acrid stuff would discourage troublemakers, at least for a while. Lopez knew that a really determined effort to break into the embassy grounds could only be slowed down, not stopped. The embassy's defenses had recently been strengthened, but they were still weak.

It became obvious at once that the demonstrators were really set on breaking in this time. Firing his M-16 into the air, using every teargas grenade he had, Lopez singlehandedly kept them outside the fence for nearly three hours. During a brief lull, while they regrouped for another try, he raced upstairs. He gathered most of the Americans in a few rooms on the upper floors and managed to sneak a few out a side door.

Then the rioters came surging in. The embassy was in their hands.

For fifty-two Americans, that day, November 4, 1979, was the first of 444 tension-filled days as hostages of the Iranian revolutionaries. Some faced an especially fearsome ordeal.

Lopez was one of those singled out for extra-harsh treatment. He spent a large part of those fourteen-and-a-half months cooped up alone, often in spaces no larger than closets. On several occasions he was badly beaten, as were several others. Afterward, when he finally got home, he told his parents, "At least I got some of the others out, right?"

Others went through experiences as grim or grimmer. Some were blindfolded and paraded through streets where the mobs screamed for their execution. Some had their hands bound for days, even weeks, while they were forced to sit in dimly lit basement rooms as long as sixteen hours a day, staring at blank walls.

In February, four months after the takeover, several male hostages were suddenly forced out of their rooms and lined up facing a wall. They could hear the click of rifle bolts as the guards seemingly prepared for a mass firing-squad execution. Then—silence. Finally, after nearly an hour of unexplained suspense, they were taken back to their rooms.

Meanwhile the U.S. government was using every available channel to negotiate with the Iranians. The situation was complicated because the Khomeini government did not have full control over the young activists in charge of the hostages. The negotiations were getting nowhere.

News of the mistreatment of the hostages leaked out.

American public opinion grew increasingly bitter. President Jimmy Carter was under tremendous pressure to take action.

At last, in April, the President gave the go-ahead signal for a rescue mission. The complex plan called for a two-day operation involving eight helicopters, six C-130 transport planes, and a detachment of specially trained anti-terrorist commandos. After a smooth start, the mission ran into disaster. Three helicopters suffered mechanical failures. A fourth collided with one of the transports on the ground in Iran and burst into flames. Eight men died. The mission had to be called back.

The Iranians were gleeful over the American failure, but furious that the rescue had even been attempted. Conditions for many of the hostages worsened for some weeks thereafter.

The negotiations began again. With agonizing slowness, a complicated deal was finally arranged. The United States made a number of reluctant concessions, most notably agreeing to return Iranian assets held in American banks.

On January 20, 1981, as America was inaugurating newly elected President Ronald Reagan, the planes carrying the hostages cleared Iranian air space and began the long journey home.

5.   The Bombers

Rue Copernic, a usually bustling street in the fashionable Passy district of Paris, was quiet for the moment. A few passersby strolled peacefully in the crisp October evening. Inside the Reform synagogue, some six hundred worshipers were celebrating the Jewish Sabbath.

The service was almost over. In a few minutes the street would fill up as the crowd came out.

With an earsplitting roar, a car parked directly across the street from the synagogue exploded. Razor-sharp, red-hot splinters of steel and glass ripped the air. Four people were killed instantly within a few feet of the car. A dozen others lay mangled and moaning.

Later the police concluded that the bomb had gone off prematurely. If it had detonated a few minutes later, as it was meant to, there would undoubtedly have been at least a hundred deaths.

Shortly after the blast there was a phone call to the official French news agency, Agence France-Presse. The caller wanted it known that his organization, the European National Fascists, claimed all credit for the action.

The date was October 4, 1980. Since 1975 over 150 violent acts had been committed in several European cities by neo-Nazi and neo-fascist groups. Many, though not all, had been directed against Jews, raking up painful memories of the Nazi past.

Two months before the Rue Copernic bombing, an exceptionally powerful bomb exploded in a railroad station in Bologna, Italy. The place was jammed with an estimated ten thousand tourists and travelers. Eighty-four died; hundreds were injured. Members of Europe's resurgent neo-Nazi movement were later prosecuted for this mass murder.

In late September, only eight days before the synagogue attack, another bomb went off at the Oktoberfest, Munich's famous annual festival. There were twelve dead and over two hundred hurt. A shadowy neo-Nazi organization known as the Military Sports Group Hoffman was believed responsible.

And a few days later, two other synagogues and two Hebrew schools were machine-gunned in France.

Indiscriminate killing seemed the hallmark of extreme right-wing terrorism. Its purpose was to spread fear throughout Western democratic society. A total disruption of normal life might open the door for a seizure of power by the self-proclaimed heirs of Hitler and Mussolini.

On October 8, four days after the incident in the Rue Copernic, the president of France made an extraordinary television appeal to his countrymen. French Jews, he declared, were "Frenchmen along with other Frenchmen," and "they shall feel recognized and treated as French as all the others."

The public's response came on October 12. For the first time since the liberation of France from Nazi occupation in 1944, representatives of all political parties marched side by side in a solemn three-hour demonstration that filled the broad avenue of the Champs-Élysées. Banners borne by the 150,000 marchers denounced anti-Semitism, every form of racism—and terrorism.

The people of France had spoken. Two years of relative peace ensued.

Then came the Israeli invasion of Lebanon in the summer of 1982. The terrorist response was not long delayed. Within a two-week period in August, Paris witnessed eight separate attacks on Jewish targets. In the raid that caused the worst bloodshed, the attackers hurled grenades into a popular Jewish restaurant and then machine-gunned customers and employees at random. Six persons died; twenty-one were wounded. Several of the victims were not Jewish. Two were American tourists. One was the restaurant's assistant chef; he was an Arab.

This time it was not neo-Nazis but an ultra-leftist group, Direct Action, that took credit for most of the bombings. A Palestinian gang named Abu Nidal was suspected of the restaurant raid.

The new wave of anti-Semitic violence was doubtless triggered by far-off events in the Middle East. But there was little question that it also reflected deep-rooted prejudices that had plagued Europe for centuries. Whether the terrorists were ultra-right, ultra-left, or Arab nationalist, the scapegoat was the same.

6. The Bank Robbers

The Brink's armored car idled outside the Nanuet shopping mall. Guard Peter Paige took up his post beside it. He hoped traffic would be light during the twenty-mile run south to New York City.

Paige's partner, Joseph Trombino, strode out of the Nanuet National Bank. Sacks of cash dangled from both hands. Under Paige's watchful eye, Trombino started to load the sacks into the armored car.

A van screeched to a halt beside them. Two men leaped out and opened fire with shotguns. A third gunman had apparently followed Trombino out; now he let fly with a 9-mm. automatic.

Paige died on the spot. Trombino fell back, clutching a shattered shoulder.

The robbers scooped up the money bags, raced to the van, and zoomed away. Their take was about $1.6 million.

The getaway vehicle pulled up half a mile away at another shopping center. The thieves abandoned the van for a small Japanese car and a U-Haul truck. They were on their way again in seconds.

But not quite fast enough. The odd switch of vehicles, with the bank sacks still conspicuous, had been noticed. Someone notified the police. By the time the robbers got to the New York State Thruway at Nyack, about five miles away, a police roadblock was in place.

The police waved the U-Haul to a halt. Somehow, the smaller vehicle had already driven through.

The white male driver and his white female companion stepped out of the U-Haul, offering no trouble. Nyack detective Arthur Keenan searched the cab: nothing. He strode around to the rear, but that door was locked. Keenan started toward the captured couple.

Several black men came storming out of the rear of the U-Haul, automatic rifles spouting lead. One Nyack policeman fell dead. Another was fatally wounded. The other officers returned fire, but they were outgunned.

The woman, unnoticed for the moment, ran toward the thruway. A passerby blocked her path. He was off-duty prison guard Michael Koch. Hearing the gunfire, he had made the instant decision to assist his brother officers. He leveled his .38-caliber revolver at her and yelled, "Don't!" She surrendered.

Glancing back, she reacted with shock to the sight of

the slain officer on the ground. "I didn't shoot him!" she shouted at Koch. Then she spotted the other robbers. Ignoring her, they were about to escape by forcing passing motorists out of their cars. Pointing at one of the thieves, she added bitterly, "He did!"

Shielded by their superior firepower, the other terrorists managed to flee. Most of them were not to remain at liberty very long.

The date of this bungled, bloody robbery was October 20, 1981. It could have been the signal for a revival of terrorist activity in the United States. Instead, it turned into disaster for the terrorists.

Behind the robbery were two radical groups dating back to the 1960s. One was the ultra-leftist revolutionary conspiracy known as the Weather Underground. Its name had been adopted from a line in a Bob Dylan song saying that no weatherman was needed to tell which way the wind was blowing. Once a widespread organization with a substantial membership, it could now claim only a small but dedicated remnant. The Weather People were almost exclusively white.

Acting with them for the first time were followers of a black radical group. These people, too, had participated in many struggles and gone through many changes since the civil rights heyday of the sixties. Now they called themselves the Black Liberation Army.

This new interracial terrorist alliance had a considerable potential for troublemaking. Funded by the loot from this one robbery, the new allies might have unleashed a nationwide wave of horror. Unpredictable numbers of recruits might have been drawn to their cause.

Terrorism throughout the world was then mounting to new climaxes of violence. In America the Weather People had gone underground in the mid-seventies. Some of their best-known leaders had since surrendered to the authorities. Outbreaks had become relatively rare. Was this sudden reappearance an evil omen for the United States in the eighties?

Spurred by the ominous possibilities, federal and local police teamed up for fast action. By the spring of 1982 ten of the most important suspects in the Brink's case were behind bars and awaiting trial.

The beast had been caged—for the time being.

THE NEW WORLDWIDE NETWORK

The terror net stretches from continent to continent, encircling the planet. Some of the linkages among terrorist groups tend to be short-lived. Others are constructed to endure.

Terrorist alliances are very often international, but they can be more than that. Some are transnational; that is, their members operate without regard to nationality or national boundaries.

All are constantly in a process of change. They expand, they shrink, they reach out for new allies, they shape new arrangements with old friends.

Some examples will convey a quick overall impression of these sometimes astonishing relationships.

October 1971. A "summit conference" of terrorist leaders from fourteen countries meets in Florence, Italy. They analyze the world situation and make plans for a revolutionary future. Periodically during the next decade, "summits" convene in such widely separated capitals as Dublin, Ireland; Lisbon, Portugal; Beirut,

19

Lebanon; Belgrade, Yugoslavia; Tripoli, Libya. The number of countries represented rises steadily.

May 1972. A three-man suicide squad from the Japanese Red Army deploys automatic rifles and grenades in a random slaughter of passengers in a waiting room at Lod airport, Israel. Two of the attackers are killed. The sole survivor declares they acted on behalf of the Popular Front for the Liberation of Palestine.

April 1974. Terrorists from Argentina, Chile, Uruguay, and Bolivia set up the Junta for Revolutionary Coordination. Its task is to plan and direct a continent-wide struggle in Latin America. Within a year the junta expands to include delegates from Colombia, Paraguay, Venezuela, and the Dominican Republic.

December 1975. A transnational terrorist band invades a meeting in Vienna, Austria, of representatives of the Organization of Petroleum Exporting Countries (OPEC). Leading the raid is the notorious Carlos the Jackal, a Venezuelan. Others in the gang include Palestinians and West Germans. They kidnap the eleven oil ministers and have them flown to Algeria. The $25 million ransom eventually collected for their release is shared by Carlos ($5 million) and the various groups within the Palestine Liberation Organization ($20 million). Carlos also gets a $2 million bonus and a villa in Libya from that country's dictator, Muammar Qaddafi.

June 1976. A crowded Air France plane is hijacked from Israel to Entebbe, Uganda. The hijackers are West Germans and Palestinians, operating with support from the Somalian, Libyan, and Ugandan governments. They separate over a hundred Jewish passengers from the others and warn that the Jews will be killed unless imprisoned terrorists are released. In a spectacular assault, Israeli paratroopers free the hostages, killing two German and five Palestinian hijackers.

July 1978. A Spanish Basque terrorist leader meets secretly in St.-Jean-de-Luz, France, with a high official of the KGB, Russia's secret police. One month later ETA, the Basque underground organization, receives three hundred Kalashnikov assault rifles and fifteen anti-tank rocket-launchers.

January 1980. A team of Turkish militants assassinates the Israeli manager of an airlines office in Istanbul. The killers had recently completed a training course run by the Palestinians in Lebanon. This is their thanks to their mentors.

May 1981. A bomb explodes in a British cultural office in Thessalonica, Greece. The terrorists who claim credit for this act are Greek, but their announced purpose is to express solidarity with the anti-British liberation struggle in Northern Ireland.

September 1981. Four members of the Armenian Secret Army for the Liberation of Armenia break into the Turkish consulate in Paris. They seize fifty hostages and demand that Turkey release all political prisoners within twelve hours. These men too have been trained in PLO camps in the Middle East. Having obtained the publicity they sought for their cause, the terrorists surrender.

March 1982. An Italian Red Brigade leader, on trial for the kidnapping of American General James L. Dozier, tells the court that Spanish, West German, and French terrorist gangs had all offered unconditional assistance after the kidnapping. The government of Bulgaria, a

Soviet satellite, had offered money and arms in exchange for NATO military secrets the general was expected to reveal.

September 1982. Italian judges issue arrest warrants for five neo-Nazis accused of the August 1980 bombing of the Bologna railroad station in which eighty-four persons died. Three of the terrorists are Italians, one an East German, one a Frenchman. They are part of an ultra-rightist network of killers for hire.

What is behind such far-reaching, at times almost contradictory alliances? What, if anything, do such seemingly different groups have in common? How tightly are they linked? Is there some super-secret central agency that controls and directs them? Is there, in short, a single underlying threat to the peace and order of the free world?

These mysteries are under constant, intensive investigation by intelligence agencies in many countries. The picture of the terrorist network that emerges is that of a loose association of independent and individualistic factions rather than of a tightly knit confederation run from a single center.

No effective plan for a coordinated worldwide terrorist offensive has ever surfaced. There has been an impressive development of mutual support and assistance systems. Such matters as the international smuggling of funds, of arms, of trainees, and of propaganda have been worked out to a high degree of efficiency. But a unified campaign of world disruption, never. Or at least, not yet.

World terrorism does have its linked centers of power, however. Large, well-equipped bases exist for training revolutionaries and guerrilla fighters as well as terrorists, and for planning and coordinating operations. Recruits flock to these camps from virtually every corner of the globe. The most important bases are located in the Soviet Union, East Germany, Czechoslovakia, Libya, South Yemen, Cuba, and Algeria. Lebanon had several major centers, run by the Palestinians, until these were wiped out in the devastating Israeli "blitz" invasion of June–August 1982. Humiliated and driven into a new exile, the Palestinians seemed likely to resort to new campaigns of terrorism.

The battles in Lebanon revealed that the international terrorist network had taken an unexpected new form. Hundreds of men captured by the Israelis were not Palestinians but mercenaries from many countries: Bangladesh, Pakistan, India, Turkey, Algeria, Syria, Jordan, Iraq, and several African nations. These hired fighters from poor countries were believed to have enlisted in the Palestine Liberation Organization more for the wages than out of any real commitment to the Palestinian cause.

The CIA and other Western intelligence agencies have long maintained close surveillance over the training camps. They have employed every conceivable means to determine who controls them. Who, for instance, selects the missions for newly graduated activists? Who identifies the targets, and who picks out the personnel for each terrorist team?

These questions all come down to one fundamental, much disputed issue: to what extent are the terrorist centers, and the intricate networks that link them, dominated by the Soviet Union?

Some experts see Russia as the chief backer and directing force behind terrorism around the world. And at least in theory, the Russians would seem to have powerful motives for sponsoring terrorism. Communism's struggle to overthrow world democracy has been going on since the 1917 revolution that put the communists into power in Russia. That struggle intensified with the outbreak of the cold war between Russia and the West in the aftermath of World War II. Any force that might help destabilize the West is a likely candidate for Russian assistance—and for Russian control if possible. Terrorism, seemingly, is just such a force.

Yet until the 1960s, the Soviet leaders appear to have shunned contact with terrorists. This policy is in accord with orthodox Marxist-Leninist doctrine, which rejects terrorism as a diversion from the "true" path of revolution. But the tumultuous sixties seemed to open tempting new possibilities for extending Soviet influence.

Rebellious young people were rioting against their governments on university campuses from Berkeley, California, to Berlin, Germany. It was the era of the increasingly unpopular Vietnam War, of "national liberation movements" erupting in former European colonies, of an emerging New Left radical movement in Western countries. To the impatient young radicals of those years, their governments seemed to block all efforts to improve the world. That impatience, that anger, provided a fertile seedbed for the growth of terrorism.

In 1968 Boris Ponomariev, Russia's director for international communist affairs, published an extraordinary article in the Soviet political quarterly *Kommunist*. Ponomariev noted that the new revolutionary upsurge included "various types of adventuristic elements," often terrorist in nature. Nevertheless, their "overall anti-imperialist direction is obvious." The Soviets must therefore cease neglecting these new radical extremists. Every effort must be made to make contact with them, to bring them under Soviet influence, to form a united front with them.

The Russians adopted the new policy at once. They began to provide secret but substantial aid to terrorist groups of many countries and political views. Soviet aid included funds, weapons, training. Inevitably the Russians began to acquire limited influence among them.

One of the leading observers of Soviet policy is Brian Jenkins, of the Rand Corporation, which works on many specialized problems for the U.S. government. Jenkins reports that Soviet aid to terrorists is never direct. It is carefully funneled through Soviet sympathizers such as Cuba, Libya, or the Palestinians. Openly acknowledged support for terrorist operations would apparently be embarrassing for the Soviet heirs of Marx and Lenin. They therefore strive to keep a low profile in terrorist circles.

The CIA has exhaustively investigated the possibility that the Soviets might gain control over world terrorism. A study completed in April 1981 concluded that there is little evidence of Soviet domination or even of Soviet attempts to stir up terrorist activity. The terrorist bands are apparently too fiercely independent for that. Each springs from a people with its own history, its own problems, its own goals. Soviet policy is of little interest to them.

Probing for possible links between the Soviets and

terrorist groupings within the United States is a responsibility of the FBI. The agency's director, William H. Webster, told a television interviewer in April 1981 that no such connections had yet been discovered.

Despite such limited results, the Soviets will undoubtedly continue to back terrorists whenever this seems advantageous to their interests. The Russians apparently believe it is better to exercise as much influence as they can among the activists, and to know at least something of their plans and intentions, than to ignore them.

The United States, too, has dabbled in the risky art of terrorist control. Covert American support has gone to anti-communist forces deemed likely to further the aims of U.S. foreign policy. Most such operations are administered through the CIA, which tries hard to manage the groups benefiting from its aid.

Best known among those with American backing are some of the anti-Castro Cuban refugee organizations with headquarters in Florida. Their biggest U.S.-sponsored operation was the disastrous 1961 attempt to invade Cuba at the Bay of Pigs. Since then thousands of young Cubans have been trained in the use of weapons and explosives for the so-called silent war against Castro. Some have also participated in operations in other islands of the Caribbean, in Central America, and even in Africa.

The determined and highly individualistic Cuban groups resist direction from the outside. Some of their actions, notably a string of assassinations of suspected pro-Castro agents in the United States, have embarrassed the American government. One out-of-control force, Omega 7, has been labeled by the FBI as the most violent terrorist organization in this country.

Terror raids by these groups against the Cuban mainland were once fairly frequent. Today, "private" expeditions against foreign territory from the United States are forbidden by federal law. American attempts to enforce this prohibition, however, may not have been entirely successful.

In 1976 the often feuding Cuban factions were persuaded to come together for a meeting in the Dominican Republic probably sponsored by the CIA. They agreed to forget their petty disputes and unite for the sake of ousting Castro. Out of this meeting came a new federation, CORU, which has been described as a Cuban PLO. One result was a series of bombings of Cuban diplomatic and airline offices throughout the Western Hemisphere.

Especially perplexing for the U.S. government has been the highly publicized Cuban involvement in organized crime. Southern Florida has long been notorious as a major center of world narcotics traffic. Prominent among those controlling it today are a number of former leaders of the U.S.-supported anti-Castro movement. As reported in a June 1982 feature story in the Long Island newspaper *Newsday,* some of these men are still occasionally employed by U.S. law-enforcement agencies as informers against suspected Castro agents and are used in other undercover roles as well. The U.S. connection has sometimes meant virtual immunity from prosecution for their criminal activities.

Whatever the extent of Soviet or American influence,

the international terror networks are a thriving and, to a surprising extent, an autonomous reality. What does the future hold for these shadowy, shifting federations? Close "fraternal" cooperation. Mutual support, in deeds as well as in words. Exchanges of men, arms, funds, intelligence information. Shared use of training facilities. Operations by transnational teams, sometimes on behalf of causes remote from the individuals participating in any given action.

The networks are spreading. The strangling fear and destruction they cause can be deadly to the world's peace. The evidence currently available indicates that they have not yet come under centralized control.

WHAT DO TODAY'S TERRORISTS WANT?

Freedom!
Independence!
Revolution!
All Power to the People!
Black Power!
White Power!
Land to the Peasants!
Ireland United!
Palestine for the Palestinians!
Save the Honor of the Nation!
Death to Traitors!
Keep Our Country Pure!
Kill the Jews!
Never Again!
God Is with Us!
In the Name of Allah!
Death to Amerika!
Down with Capitalism! (Communism! Imperialism!
   Socialism! Racism! Zionism! Fascism!)

Words, mere words. But across the world there exist thousands of men and women willing to die for words like these. Or kill for them. Or terrorize innocent people for them.

Even a list as long as the one above provides only a brief sampling. The causes that inspire terrorism today are bewildering in their variety. A full list would reflect an incredible range of nationalities, religions, languages, histories, political philosophies. In a few instances it would reflect only the mental derangement of fanatical leaders.

Some of these slogans express legitimate aspirations for change. Organized political movements throughout the world are struggling to win popular support for such goals by legal and peaceable means. When small groups of frustrated radical extremists seize upon grievances like these and plunge into violence, however, society is confronted by terrorism.

Virtually all terrorists engage in certain typical forms of behavior:

- the use or the threat of violence
- the use of fear to attain temporary power over authorities
- the demand for rapid, radical political change
- the selection of targets likely to arouse maximum media attention, bringing maximum public pressure on the authorities (as one expert puts it, "Terrorism is theater")
- the selection of weak or vulnerable targets, capable of being overpowered and controlled by the terrorists' limited armed force.

The CIA pointed out in a 1980 report that terrorists may be "acting for, or in opposition to, established governmental authority." In other words, not all terrorism is anti-government. It is sometimes sponsored by governments. This is most commonly done by funding, arming, and training activists for operations outside the sponsoring country. In 1980 alone twenty-four countries are known to have backed systematic campaigns of assassination against their political enemies abroad.

Today's world also includes a number of governments that direct violence against their own people to intimidate and silence any political opposition. This is known as "state terrorism." Countries where it is common include Libya, Iran, Argentina, Chile, Guatemala, the Soviet Union, and some of its satellites in Eastern Europe. When the government of South Africa uses violence against the black majority to enforce its racist policy of apartheid, it too is practicing state terrorism.

A special characteristic of terrorist operations carried out by groups other than governments, the CIA notes, is that they "are intended to shock or intimidate a target group wider than the immediate victims." As an example, the real target of a skyjacking is not the group of hostages in the airliner, but rather a government.

Terrorism differs from both revolution and guerrilla warfare. A full-scale revolution requires large and reasonably well organized forces, reinforced by broad popular support. The revolutionists must be able to mount a direct armed challenge to the established power.

Guerrilla war, too, requires strong forces and the

people's support. But guerrilla detachments are usually too small and too ill-armed for all-out confrontation with the armed might available to governments. Theirs is a hit-and-run style of war. Between operations they disappear among the population, subsisting on its aid and encouragement.

Terrorism differs from both in that its forces are much smaller in number and military capability and its relationship to the people is much more remote. The activists often regard themselves as a glamorous, elite group setting an example of revolutionary heroism for the people to emulate. They devote little or no effort to the slow, tedious, humdrum task of working with the common people to educate and organize them.

They may have tried and found the people unresponsive to their overheated propaganda. They become alienated and isolated from the people. Terrorists operate with such limited popular support that their attacks can only be sporadic and directed against targets carefully chosen for their inability to resist small-group assaults.

The difference was well stated by William P. Lineberry in his 1977 study, *The Struggle against Terrorism*: "Revolution, like war, is the strategy of the strong. Terrorism is the strategy of the weak."

A clear distinction should also be made between terrorism and mere criminal behavior. For example, in 1977 and 1978 a total of fifty-five aircraft were hijacked worldwide. Only eight of these hijackings had any political purpose. The others were intended only to extort money from the airlines or to escape from pursuing lawmen.

What Do Today's Terrorists Want?   33

A unique case made headlines in 1981. Four heavily armed men seized control of the Polish embassy in Berne, Switzerland. They held more than a dozen people hostage for three days. Playing the role of political terrorists, they at first demanded that the Polish government end martial law and release all political prisoners. Later they revealed their real aim: $1.4 million in ransom and safe passage out of Switzerland. Specially trained Swiss police officers eventually stormed the embassy, freed the hostages, and captured all four criminals.

Most experts agree that terrorist causes can be classified into two main types, with numerous minor variations and considerable overlapping among them.

One broad category is termed "nationalist-separatist." Extremists of this type represent nations, national minorities, ethnic or racial groups fighting for freedom from what they regard as foreign rule. Examples include Northern Ireland's IRA, the Spanish Basques' ETA, the Palestine Liberation Organization, the anti-Turkish Armenian groups, the African National Congress in South Africa, the French-speaking activists of Canada's province of Quebec, and, in the United States, the Puerto Rican FALN.

The second major class of terrorists is based on political ideology. This is a complicated category with several subgroups. The largest of these is formed by the various extremist forces of the radical left. These include revolutionary socialists and communists of various persuasions: Trotskyites, Maoists, Castroites; admirers of Che Guevara and Ho Chi Minh; followers of such ultra-

LOURDES HIGH SCHOOL LIBRARY
4034 W. 56TH STREET
CHICAGO, ILLINOIS 60629

leftist writers as Frantz Fanon, Carlos Marighella, and Herbert Marcuse.

The young people who form the majority in most left-wing terrorist groups almost always start out with high ideals. They are moved by genuine injustices in the society around them, such as poverty, racism, unemployment, and war.

Typically they first seek to fight these injustices through peaceable reform movements. In countries where democratic avenues for change appear closed or where official resistance to change is powerful, the young become impatient and turn to extremist violence.

In theory the ultra-leftists all agree that the established order is evil and oppressive and must be violently overthrown. The trouble is that their writing and public statements are strikingly vague as to exactly what kind of society should replace the existing one. An example is the sixty-page pamphlet, "Resolution on Strategic Direction," published by the Italian Red Brigades in 1978. Only four lines in the entire statement deal with the future society that is supposedly the group's ultimate goal.

Revolutionists of the ultra-left often preach some unspecified form of "socialism" as their objective. But with their contempt for all authority, they are much closer in spirit to anarchism. Anarchists view all government as a vicious conspiracy for oppressing the people.

Groups fitting into the ultra-left category have included West Germany's Baader-Meinhof Gang and Red Army Faction, Italy's Red Brigades and Armed Proletarian Cells, Argentina's ERP and Montoneros, Uruguay's Tupamaros, the Japanese Red Army, the Turkish

People's Liberation Army, and America's Weather Underground, New World Liberation Front, and Black Liberation Army. Some of these—notably the Argentine and Uruguayan bands, Baader-Meinhof, and the Weather Underground—have been either driven into exile or badly crippled during the past decade.

The left-wing terrorist category does not, however, include most orthodox communists. Official communist doctrine rejects terrorism. The orthodox communist parties have traditionally regarded terrorists with suspicion and contempt, deriding them as adventurists, romantic individualists, unstable elements, and infantile extremists.

Karl Marx, founder of modern communism, opposed terrorist acts by individuals or small groups. The true revolutionist, Marx wrote, must concentrate on the central task of preparing the masses for participation in the revolutionary struggle. V. I. Lenin, leader of the Russian revolution and founder of the Soviet state, asserted that terrorism only "diverts the most active fighters from their real task." Terrorist operations, Lenin insisted, "have nothing in common with the forcible actions of the people's revolution."

In the opinion of left-wing extremists dedicated to the violent overthrow of democratic countries, the official communist parties are "traitors to the cause," "bourgeois revisionists," "filthy sellouts." Only they, the terrorists, uphold the true cause of violent revolution.

At the opposite end of the political spectrum are the right-wing extremists. Like the leftists, they aspire to the violent overthrow of established democratic governments. But far from espousing any form of socialism or communism, they favor ultra-nationalistic dictatorships or police states, like those that once ruled Nazi Germany or fascist Italy. Rightists despise democracy as a "decadent" way of life, and they oppose most forms of social progress or reform.

Believed to be the largest of these gangs is the European National Fascist Union, which has been especially active in France and Belgium. Others include West Germany's Military Sports Group Hoffman; Italy's Black Order, Armed Revolutionary Nuclei, and National Advanced Guard; Yugoslavia's Croatian Revolutionary Brotherhood; and Spain's Youth Force and oddly named Warriors of Christ the King. America, too, is represented, with the Ku Klux Klan, American Nazi Party, Jewish Defense League, and such anti-Castro Cuban groups as Omega 7.

Still another terrorist category is composed of groups whose ideology is profoundly religious as well as political. One of the oldest such groups in the Middle East is the Muslim Brotherhood. Active over the past four decades, this widespread and powerfully entrenched organization has been responsible for dozens of bombings and assassinations aimed at Muslim officials condemned for allegedly straying from the path of strict obedience to sacred Koranic law. President Anwar Sadat of Egypt was only one of the brotherhood's latest victims.

Also deeply rooted in religious conflict is the long and bitter conflict in Northern Ireland. Here the Roman Catholic minority is pitted against the dominant Protestant majority. Catholic militants are organized into the two wings of the Irish Republican Army, an experienced and dreaded force. In recent years most IRA violence has been the work of its so-called Provisional wing, whose members are familiarly known as the Provos. The Official wing has appeared more ready to negotiate some sort of political compromise.

As ruthless as the Provos are their deadly rivals, the Protestant terrorists of the Ulster Defense Association. The intensity of Protestant feeling was mirrored in a dramatic statement published in Dublin in 1973. We can beat the IRA, it declared,

> but how can we be expected to beat the world revolutionary movement which supplies arms and training . . . to the IRA?
>
> We do not have large funds from overindulgent sentimentally sick Irishmen in America who send the funds of capitalism to sow communism here. . . . Send the politicians and the officers home and leave us the men and the weapons . . . and we will send you the IRA wrapped up in little boxes and little tins like cans of baked beans.

Clear classification of the world's terrorist organizations is complicated by the fact that some of them fit more than one category. This is particularly true for several of the nationalist-separatist groups.

The Popular Front for the Liberation of Palestine is typical of these dual-purpose organizations. Its name seems to mark it merely as a nationalist body seeking to regain its homeland. But the PFLP is also deeply imbued with the ideology of Marxism-Leninism, or communism. PFLP founder George Habash has made this clear on many occasions: "Our enemy is not just Israel. . . . Our revolution is a phase of world revolution." The PFLP platform echoes this theme: "The Palestinian struggle is a part of the whole Arab liberation movement and of the world liberation movement."

Similar influences have been at work among the Basques, Armenians, Africans, Puerto Ricans, and other nationalist groups.

Irish Americans, whose financial support has long been the principal source of IRA funding, may be surprised to learn of the IRA's actual goals. Both its Official and its Provisional wings aspire to create an Ireland that will be not only free and united but also socialist. Understandably, this revolutionary goal is soft-pedaled by IRA spokesmen on fund-raising trips in the United States.

Even harder to classify are the Armenian terrorists. One of their main forces, the Armenian Secret Army for the Liberation of Armenia, seems to have typical nationalist-separatist objectives. ASALA demands the separation of an area in northeastern Turkey to form a national homeland for the Armenian inhabitants. Some ASALA activists are known to have received their training in the Palestinian camps of the Middle East.

The goals of the other major Armenian terrorist band have a different focus. The Justice Commandos for the Armenian Genocide seek to compel the Turkish government to acknowledge and pay compensation for a mass murder allegedly committed in 1915. They accuse the Turks of wantonly and deliberately murdering nearly a million and a half Armenians at that time. The Armenians insist that this genocidal action is comparable to the Nazi extermination of the Jews during World War II, but has received much less attention. They refer to it as "the forgotten genocide."

The Turks have always denied that any such event ever happened. Most historians believe that the available evidence supports the Armenians' claims, although there may be some question as to the exact number of victims.

Whatever the historical truth, there can be no doubt about the dimensions of Armenian terrorism. These forces have perpetrated nearly 150 bombings and assassinations during the past decade, in locations ranging from Sydney, Australia, to Los Angeles, Boston, Washington, and many of the capitals of Europe. Over twenty Turkish diplomats have been murdered since 1975.

The Armenians' most horrendous attack came in August 1982. A three-man suicide squad opened up with bombs and machine guns at Ankara airport. Six persons were killed and about 250 wounded. It was the first Armenian operation within Turkey. The raiders warned other countries of similar attacks to come if Armenian demands were not met.

A moral problem underlying the Armenian terrorism has troubled many. What ethical justification can there be for an assassination campaign against persons who were not even born when this seventy-year-old crime was committed?

Some observers have noted an even more disturbing trend among certain terrorist elements. *New York Times* writer Flora Lewis, for instance, sees some groups as becoming so desperate, so used to senseless violence, so cynical, that they have virtually abandoned whatever idealistic hopes and plans they may once have harbored for the future. They seem now to kill and destroy without logical purpose.

Walter Laqueur, a widely respected authority, notes that terrorist movements once "took pride in elaborate ideological justifications, but this is no longer so." Instead, they seem increasingly influenced by the philosophy of pure destructiveness known as nihilism, which justifies savaging the established order without regard to what may follow.

A troubling example is the Weather Underground's failed robbery of the Brink's armored car in October 1981. Considering the utter failure of this group's decade-long effort to spark some sort of revolutionary movement among the American people, it is hard to see any sensible political purpose for the robbery. It is impossible to make any sense at all of the robbers' shooting of the two guards without any warning and in spite of the fact that the guards made no attempt at resistance. Such actions can evoke only anger and revulsion among the very people the terrorists supposedly seek to lead.

What constructive aim could possibly have been achieved by the Puerto Rican FALN terrorists when they bombed Fraunces Tavern in downtown New York City, the place where George Washington bade farewell to his officers two hundred years ago? What sympathy could be won from the American people by a mindless act that killed four innocent people and almost destroyed one of the nation's revered patriotic shrines?

Similar questions have to be asked of the neo-fascists who pointlessly murdered close to a hundred innocent travelers in the August 1980 bombing of the Bologna railroad station; of the anti-Castro Cubans who planted a bomb aboard a Cubana Airways plane and killed seventy-three persons; of the Muslim Brotherhood men who planted a bomb in a car on a busy Damascus street in November 1981, killing ninety passersby, including thirty-one women and children; of the Turkish fanatic who attempted to assassinate Pope John Paul II in the midst of a throng of worshipers in St. Peter's Square in Rome in May 1981; of the five young Arabs who hurled incendiary bombs into a Pan American World Airways plane at the Rome airport in 1973, burning thirty-two passengers to death; and of those who committed acts of senseless savagery too numerous to list.

Positive, humane goals for acts such as these are hardly conceivable. But there is an explanation. It sheds a horrific light on the twisted reasoning behind much of the terrorism of our time.

The purpose of such deliberate horror is to disrupt democratic societies to such a point that, amid the chaos, the authorities have no alternative but to adopt the harshest, most repressive countermeasures.

As Brazilian terrorist leader Carlos Marighella wrote in his *Handbook of Urban Guerrilla Warfare*, the state must be driven to "unbearable persecution" of all who question it in any way. Ulrike Meinhof, cofounder of West Germany's infamous Baader-Meinhof Gang, urged unrestrained and intentionally shocking violence in order to bring out "the latent fascism in society." Red Brigades' founder Renato Curcio incited "working-class terror" to provoke the government "to re-establish control by intensified repression and progressive militarization of the state."

The theory underlying this almost incredible policy is that, in the face of such drastic action by their government, the people will naturally and inevitably turn to the terrorists for leadership. The dream of revolution will then be realized, and the as yet unspecified new society established.

Reality has proved this theory false many times. One example is the harsh authoritarian regimes now ruling most of South America. At least three of these military dictatorships—those in Brazil, Argentina, and Uruguay—came to power as a direct response to intensive terrorist campaigns that were so successful for a time that they threatened to cause a total breakdown of social order. Far from leading to an upsurge of popular support for the terrorists, the results were the relentless destruction of their forces in these countries and exile for the few surviving leaders.

In Turkey the circumstances were slightly different, but the results were the same. By the late 1970s the country was in a virtual state of civil war. According to a 1981 report by the U.S. Senate Subcommittee on Security and Terrorism:

> The excesses of the communist terrorists created a backlash from the extreme right. Both leftist and rightist groups were heavily armed and challenged each other in the streets, on the campuses, in the cafes.

There were large-scale massacres, the report stated, "in many towns and villages." The country's military leaders took over the Turkish government on September 12, 1980. By that time "the daily rate of killing had attained an unbelievable twenty-eight lives."

With the establishment of a military dictatorship, order was restored. The death toll dropped to less than one a day.

But if there had been a gain in security, there was also a loss of liberty. Some 45,000 persons have been arrested. For a time, terrorist suspects were executed on the spot. This practice has apparently been stopped, but many accused persons have died in jail. Torture is supposedly not encouraged officially, but 342 legal charges of torture and brutality have been filed against the police and the military. At least twenty police officers have been prosecuted on these charges.

The news media are totally controlled by those in power. All demonstrations, political meetings, and strikes have been banned. One government decree even required male students to wear their hair short and shave off their beards.

If repression was the goal of the terrorists, it was hardly likely to win the support of the people.

One final example will further illuminate the devious terrorist mentality. The most active terrorist group in Spain today is ETA, the nationalist-separatist and Marxist organization of the Basques. It not only refuses to accept Spain's new democratic government but also has publicly threatened to execute Basques who collaborate with it. ETA's uncompromising goal: total secession from Spain and the establishment of an independent and "socialist" Basque nation. There is considerable certainty that only a tiny minority of the Basque people favor this drastic step.

In the summer of 1979 the Spanish government negotiated with other Basque representatives a "Statute of Basque Autonomy." It would grant almost all of the Basques' demands: they could freely study and speak their own language, use their own flag, set up their own schools and courts, but the Basque region would remain a part of Spain. ETA's response was a renewed and intensified wave of violence.

The Basque National Council, which represents all political parties, states flatly that all ETA really wants is to "block peaceful coexistence, foment mutual distrust, and provoke a military coup d'etat." The Spanish communist party, too, has denounced the group. Communist leader Manuel Azcarate asserts that ETA "wants the prisons overflowing with Basques again, screams from the torture chambers."

One of the terrorists' own favorite authors, Herbert Marcuse, has spoken for many who have been repelled by such tactics: "Their methods are not those of liberation."

But the most damning admission of all came from among the terrorists themselves. On trial in Rome for the 1981 kidnapping of U.S. General James L. Dozier, Red Brigade leader Antonio Savasta circulated a statement that was almost pathetic in its honesty. He admitted that he and his comrades had behaved like "pure adventurists, representatives of the most infantile extremism." They must stop now; otherwise they would "crush everything."

Another Red Brigade ideologist wrote from his prison cell that "the armed struggle failed in all the political and social goals it had set for itself for ten years." The extremists must now "have the courage to refuse it totally." To continue would mean only that "one condemns oneself to madness."

IV.

TRAINING AND ARMING FOR TERROR

Today the "Molotov cocktail" is still the most commonly used of all weapons of terrorism. Its name stems from the device's first use by Russian guerrillas fighting the Germans in World War II. No extensive training or knowledge is needed either to make it or to use it.

It is simply a glass bottle filled with gasoline. The final ingredient: a little daring. The attacker must get to within throwing range of the target, touch a lighted match to the fuse, throw the device, and—get away fast!

Cheap. Easy to make. In certain situations devastatingly effective. That is why the Molotov cocktail is still so popular among the impoverished, the untrained, the amateurs of terrorism.

But such primitive weapons are obviously of limited usefulness. The full scope of modern terrorist activity requires rigorous training, broad knowledge, technical sophistication, and a wide variety of armament.

Terrorism's requirements are spelled out in detail in the so-called minimanual, a little book that has become a

45

kind of bible of terrorism. Its formal title is *Handbook of Urban Guerrilla Warfare* (modern terrorists prefer to be called urban guerrillas). The author, Carlos Marighella, led a Brazilian terrorist gang in the 1960s. Killed in a police ambush in Sao Paulo in 1969, Marighella is venerated as a martyr among terrorists.

In the minimanual, Marighella addresses himself first to the attitude that must be inculcated into the would-be terrorist. He must be trained

> to stand up against fatigue, hunger, rain, heat. To know how to hide and be vigilant. To conquer the art of dissembling. Never to fear danger. To behave the same by day as by night. Not to act impetuously. To have unlimited patience. To remain calm and cool in the worst conditions and situations. Never to leave a track or trail. Not to get discouraged.

The terrorist must master the skills of driving cars at high speed, piloting aircraft, handling boats. He must understand mechanics, know how to maintain and operate radio equipment, understand the mysteries of electricity and electronics. He should be able to read maps and use topographical instruments. Some knowledge of chemistry and a sound basic introduction to modern medicine are indispensable. Finally, the trainee must of course be experienced in handling all kinds of weapons and must understand explosives.

As Marighella puts it, the terrorist's "reason for existence . . . is to shoot." He must therefore be trained "to shoot well," for he will often face situations in which he will have "to shoot first and he cannot err in his shot."

Another manual widely used for instructing terrorist

recruits dates back to World War II. This is an illustrated British pamphlet, thousands of copies of which were dropped by parachute to the anti-Nazi resistance forces in countries occupied by the Germans. Written in five languages, it conveys clear, step-by-step directions on such specialized matters as how and when to sabotage a railway line, how to attack an enemy installation with only a small force, and how to use recently invented plastic explosives.

Many copies of this handy thirty-two-page guide doubtless survived the war and found their way into the hands of today's terrorists. Recent terrorist manuals often include whole sections based on the pamphlet.

During training, every effort is made to rupture the trainee's former ties with friends and family. Among Argentina's Montoneros, for example, the trainee would be asked at one point what he would do if his mother were arrested by the enemy. The only correct answer: "I would do nothing."

The new recruit is put through lengthy "rap sessions" in which a single way of thinking is drilled into him. He is permitted not the slightest chance to compare the new ideas with others or with his own experience. When he has progressed far enough, he will often be given a new name, carefully chosen to symbolize the revolutionary cause. He may, for instance, be named after a dead terrorist or some revolutionary hero of the past.

Having turned away from his past life, the recruit will then be expected to pledge absolute loyalty to his new comrades. There is only one way to fulfill this pledge: instant, automatic, unquestioning obedience to any and every order he receives.

For full acceptance into some Latin American groups, recruits must commit an irrevocable act that will brand them forever as outcasts from society. That act is the cold-blooded killing of a policeman or soldier.

Terrorist trainees today receive their instruction in one of a chain of camps that extends from the Soviet Union through its satellites in Eastern Europe, through the Middle East and North Africa to Cuba. Thousands of men and women from every part of the world have passed through these camps in the last fifteen to twenty years.

Obviously not all trainees become active terrorists. Many simply return home to join some existing revolutionary party or movement, often to assume a leadership role. In countries where large-scale guerrilla warfare is already under way, some enlist for combat. But many hundreds do immediately commit themselves as full-fledged terrorists.

The training they receive has been of variable quality. Much depends on the length of time they stay and on the qualifications of their instructors. Some centers in the Middle East are notorious for the low level of their programs. Trainees sometimes visit only for a few weeks, barely absorbing the most elementary ideas and techniques.

A ludicrous example was the preparation that a group of Egyptians received at one of the huge camps in Libya. They belonged to an organization seeking to overthrow the Egyptian government. In the Libyan camp they were supposedly trained to infiltrate back across the border into their own country, to make their way back to Cairo, and to assassinate several top leaders. The Egyptian authorities picked them up almost as soon as they crossed the border. They were carrying identical suitcases supplied by their mentors, Libyan as well as Egyptian money, and similar weapons, and they were still wearing Libyan army underpants.

Unbelievable as it may seem, some of the Libyan camps featured American instructors. In a sensational series of articles published in *The New York Times* in June 1981, investigative reporter Seymour Hersh revealed that two former CIA agents, Frank E. Terpil and Edwin P. Wilson, had set up a profitable but illegal business of selling arms and expertise for the use of Libyan terrorists. They also hired former members of the U.S. Army's elite Green Beret force, to "set up a training school and teach the Libyans the latest techniques in assassination and international terror."

Terpil and Wilson were indicted in 1980 for illegally shipping twenty tons of plastic explosive to Libya three years earlier. They were in hiding abroad at the time of the indictment, but Wilson was lured back to the United States and arrested in June 1982 as a result of a ruse engineered by the U.S. Department of Justice. He was convicted in November 1982 of several charges of illegal gun sales, with more charges pending against him.

The story of how they recruited a Green Beret instructor with long experience in covert operations and several former Green Berets makes up what *The New York Times* called "one of the strangest and most disturbing operations in the annals of international espionage."

Both the CIA and the U.S. Army have officially denied authorizing any such operation. But according to a feature story by Phillip Taubman in *The New York Times*

Magazine, July 4, 1982, senior officials of the CIA may have given approval "perhaps in the hope it would produce valuable information on Libyan terrorism." There is also a suspicion that these officials "might have been silent partners of Wilson."

As for the Green Berets, they apparently believed that higher authority had okayed their mission as a way of penetrating the Libyan espionage system. They made some efforts to check this. Wilson's highly placed friends in the CIA and the Defense Department may have intercepted their inquiries.

In any case, the group arrived in the Libyan capital of Tripoli in August 1977. They brought considerable specialized military equipment, plus "several bags filled with technical manuals and blueprints of advanced electronic equipment." They were surprised to meet a number of American weapons experts who were serving as instructors. At least one of the new arrivals, Luke Thompson, then still a member of the Green Berets, found after some weeks that he could not justify helping the Libyan terrorists. He left shortly thereafter.

High-level investigations by several U.S. government agencies, with Thompson as one of the key witnesses, were soon under way. The indictments of Terpil and Wilson were only the tip of the iceberg. The essential question was how such an elaborate program of aid to a hostile country's terrorist operations could have been encouraged by such high-ranking officials. Shock waves were spreading throughout the U.S. intelligence community.

Although there are grounds for doubt about the overall effectiveness of the training at some of the Libyan camps, the situation is different elsewhere.

Probably the most thorough training courses are those given in the Soviet Union. They last as long as six months. Detailed descriptions have been obtained from Palestinians trained there who were later captured by the Israelis.

A typical day in a Soviet camp begins at 5:00 A.M. An hour of gymnastics and a morning parade precede breakfast. The meal is followed by two hours of political studies which, for obvious reasons, emphasize the greatness and achievements of the Soviet Union. Subjects studied include Marxism-Leninism, Soviet history, anti-imperialism, Zionism as a form of imperialism, and so on.

In the afternoon the trainees go through three hours of practical courses. These cover such matters as the use of mines and other explosives, commando field tactics, urban guerrilla tactics, and, above all, comprehensive training in marksmanship and the handling of weapons.

The Cuban camps, too, are believed to offer effective training. They follow the Soviet model to some extent, and some of their instructors are Russian. But the Cubans can draw on their own successful guerrilla experience. Cuban instructors are especially popular among Third World guerrilla movements such as those of Central and South America, where the problems are similar to those overcome by the Cuban revolutionaries. Experienced Cuban instructors teach not only in their own country but also in many of the Middle Eastern and North African camps.

Trainees in large numbers started to come to Cuba from Western Europe and the United States in the tumultuous 1960s. By the late 1970s some 2,500 young Americans had trained in these camps. They usually arrived during summer vacations, calling themselves the Venceremos ("We will win") Brigades. Some of them later put their newly acquired skills to work as members of the Weather Underground and other radical groups in the United States.

Within the United States, terrorist training had to be carried out under the stressful conditions of the underground life. Constantly pursued and harassed by law-enforcement authorities, the American groups often operated in isolation from one another, out of touch with the public and with normal living. In "The Seeds of Terror," a feature story in *The New York Times Magazine*, November 22, 1981, Lucinda Franks described how the Weather Underground tried to shape itself into a "street-fighting guerrilla force." Acting on advice from a Vietnamese communist they had met in Cuba, the Weather People broke up into "collectives" of ten to twenty men and women. Their training procedures were sometimes extreme:

> In order to get rid of bourgeois habits, the collectives forced couples to separate, required homosexuality, drug-taking, and round-the-clock sessions of self-criticism. One time, they skinned and ate an alley-cat. . . . Often rising at dawn, they would practice karate, train at rifle clubs, and . . . work out how they would grapple with police and where they would kick them. Part of the day was devoted to the study of political literature.

No matter how varied the training program, sooner or later it must focus on the one most essential subject of all: weapons training. The weapons to be mastered by the well-trained terrorist constitute a formidable and constantly improving arsenal.

To be suited for terrorist use, weapons must meet certain specifications. They must be readily and cheaply available; simple to make, maintain, and operate; dependable and efficient; sufficiently powerful to do the job; lightweight and compact enough to be easily concealed.

The easiest weapon for terrorists to acquire is a crude homemade explosive created from some easily available material. The Molotov cocktail is one example. Another simple explosive can be made from any nitrogen-rich fertilizer mixed with diesel oil, though this can sometimes be hard to detonate. The Weather Underground used a truckload of this material to blow up the Army Mathematics Center at the University of Wisconsin in 1970.

Would-be bombers obtain commercially manufactured explosives in a number of ways. Dynamite, for example, can be stolen from construction sites, mines, or quarries. Military explosives are pilfered from armed-forces bases, government arsenals, or hijacked military vehicles. Hand grenades are particularly sought after. Both the U.S. Army's M-26 grenade and the Soviet Army's RGD-5 have done murderous work for terrorists. These are fragmentation grenades designed strictly for anti-personnel purposes. For other uses, the military plastic explosive is even more strongly favored. It is easy to carry, conceal, and use, and it can be shaped to fit almost any target.

The militants are trained to detonate these materials by all the usual methods: chemical or electrical detonators, flame, physical pressure. Specialized electronic devices require higher levels of skill.

A noteworthy example is the method used by an Israeli "hit team" that called itself "the Wrath of God" to assassinate Mahmoud Hamshari, a top PLO official, in Paris in 1972. He was known to have helped plan the Munich massacre in which eleven Israeli athletes competing in the Olympic Games that year were taken hostage and eventually killed. The Israelis tracked Hamshari to a hotel in Paris. Then they rigged the telephone in his room. Waiting until his wife and children were out and he was alone, they phoned him, made certain the speaker was indeed Hamshari, and electronically triggered the explosive they had placed in the phone.

Another specialized type of bomb that came into wide use in the 1970s was the letter bomb, or parcel bomb. This was an innocent-looking piece of mail containing small but lethal explosive charges. The most frequent form of detonator was a "mousetrap" mechanism that sprang shut, closing an electrical circuit, when the envelope flap or parcel lid was lifted.

The letter bomb was the brainchild of Ahmed Jibril, a former Syrian army captain trained in terrorism by the Soviets. He headed a small Palestinian force known as the Popular Front for the Liberation of Palestine— General Command. Jibril's group mailed dozens, perhaps hundreds, of letter bombs to Israeli diplomatic posts and Zionist leaders around the world. The results were deadly. The idea was widely imitated for a time, even by the Israelis. Postal authorities have since developed improved detection methods, and these devices are no longer in common use.

Jibril is also credited with the idea of placing small bombs inside portable radios and cassette players. His favorite technique was to have young Palestinians seek out and befriend European girls planning a trip on an airline marked as a target of violence. They would spend an enjoyable few hours or even days together. The girls would be handed the "gifts" by their charming boyfriends just before boarding the aircraft, totally unaware of their destructive contents.

Some terrorists make frequent use of incendiary bombs, which set fires and cause blast damage as well. The IRA, for example, has developed a simple but deadly incendiary consisting of a small bomb surrounded by cans of gasoline.

Also popular among terrorists are car bombs. These can contain as much as 200 pounds of explosive. Planted in a car parked in front of a store or building, they have often been spectacularly effective. Car bombs can also be rigged with remote-control devices so that they can be detonated precisely when some selected individual or group is passing.

This technique was used with especially shocking effect on July 20, 1982. A remote-controlled IRA car bomb killed three members of the Queen's Household Cavalry and several horses on parade near Buckingham Palace in London. Twenty-three others were injured. The weapon's maiming power was augmented by studding it with hundreds of four- and five-inch nails.

Once alerted to the presence of a suspicious vehicle, police usually have little difficulty locating and defusing car bombs. Specially trained dogs are often brought in to sniff out the explosive. The bombers' response has been to rig car bombs with booby traps, making removal extremely dangerous.

Guns used for terrorist purposes have their own special requirements. The basic choice between single-shot, semiautomatic, or fully automatic weapons will obviously depend on whether the plan involves sharpshooting at a single target or spraying a group from a distance.

The preferred automatic weapons are those whose rate of fire is not too rapid, since ammunition supplies are likely to be limited on most operations. Also desirable in a terrorist gun is good stopping power, to ensure that the victim not only will go down but will also be unable to return fire.

Most of the favored guns are military weapons. These are supposedly available only to regular armed forces and law-enforcement authorities, but the major terrorist groups have had little difficulty in accumulating ample stocks. Quantities can be purchased through black-market dealers or even on the open market. The illegal arms traffic is a billion-dollar business today.

Another source of weapons is sympathetic governments, which can often be counted on to share their supplies. Raids on military bases, police stations, arsenals, and even private gun clubs have also enriched the revolutionaries' armories. In a world where nations are constantly at war or preparing for war, there is no shortage of the very finest weapons for the taking.

Three basic types of automatic weapons are in common use today: the assault or automatic rifle, the submachine gun, and the machine pistol. Among the automatic rifles, two are favored by terrorists. One is Soviet-made, the other American.

The Soviet model is the Kalashnikov AK-47, now found in enormous numbers among militant groups the world over. The Kalashnikov is much admired for its exceptional reliability even under the worst conditions of dirt, mud, heat, or moisture. Its simplicity of design makes it ideal for ill-trained or partly trained terrorists. The Kalashnikov's curved magazine holds thirty rounds of 7.62-mm. ammunition. It has a high muzzle velocity of 2,330 feet per second, for strong stopping power.

The American assault rifle preferred by some terrorist groups is the Armalite AR-18. It has been a particular favorite with the IRA. The Armalite's special feature is the unmatched velocity of its bullets: 3,250 feet per second. Their penetration power is such that they can pierce medium steel plate, bulletproof vests, and steel helmets at a range of 500 yards. Even a minor wound inflicted by an Armalite can be fatal, because of its shock power. The weapon's one handicap is that its length (36.38 inches) makes it hard to conceal. The Armalite carries twenty rounds of relatively small-caliber 5.56-mm. ammunition.

Substantial quantities of the American M-16, the U.S. Army's basic infantry weapon, have recently turned up in PLO hands. Similar to the Armalite in many respects, the M-16 suffers from one troublesome characteristic: it tends to jam when dirty or wet. Most terrorists are ill-equipped to deal with jammed weapons.

Submachine guns are used only occasionally by today's terrorists. Most models are too big and unwieldy, and they are regarded as old-fashioned.

One model that is still brought into play from time to time by the IRA is the old .45-caliber Thompson submachine gun, or tommy gun. This American-made weapon, with its magazine in the form of an instantly recognizable circular drum, was first made infamous in the gangster wars of 1920s. It was copied and widely used by the Russians during World War II. Today's models are somewhat improved, but it remains basically the same weapon.

Much lighter and simpler is the 9-mm. British-made Sten submachine gun. Some two million of these were manufactured during World War II. Many thousands were parachuted to the resistance forces in Nazi-occupied Europe, and it still appears occasionally in the hands of European terrorists. The Sten gun has some dangerous characteristics. It tends to fire, for instance, if the butt hits the ground.

The machine pistol is basically a miniature version of the submachine gun. Terrorists prefer one model over all others: the Skorpion VZ-61, made in Czechoslovakia. Its small bulk, light weight, and deadly effect at close range make it the ideal assassination weapon. Former Italian Prime Minister Aldo Moro was put to death by his Red Brigade kidnappers in 1978 with eleven slugs fired from a Skorpion. The Skorpion magazine holds from ten to twenty rounds of .32-caliber or 7.65-mm. ammunition.

The revolver has stood alongside the bomb as the traditional weapon of terrorists for over a hundred years. Today's terrorists have a wide choice. The most powerful revolver by far is the Astra .357 Magnum. The wounds it inflicts are so horrendous that victims rarely survive. Closely rivaling it are the American-made Browning high-power pistol, which features a thirteen-round magazine, and the Czech M-52, which fires an extra-powerful cartridge. The Soviets manufacture two reliable models, the Makarov and the Tokarev, that are widely used by the world's many Russian-supplied terrorist bands. West European terrorists seem to favor the all-purpose, German-made Walther P-38.

A whole new spectrum of terrorist possibilities has been opened in recent years with the development of PGMs, or Precision Guided Munitions. These are rocket launchers whose missiles can be guided or redirected in flight, either by their own built-in guidance systems or by the individual firing the weapon. Many are so light and compact that they can be carried and fired by one or two persons. They have an effective range of several kilometers.

The best-known example is the surface-to-air missile, for anti-aircraft use. Terrorist arsenals are known to include the American Redeye and its successor the Stinger, the Soviet SAM-7 Strela, and the British Blowpipe. Each of these hand-held, shoulder-borne weapons fires a missile that carries an infrared guidance system and heat-seeing sensors. Once these devices have locked on to any heat-emitting source, such as a jet airplane's exhaust, the missile will pursue the aircraft through all sorts of evasive maneuvers until it homes in for the kill.

In 1973 the Rome police arrested five Arabs who had rented an apartment strategically located just under the flight path of airliners taking off from Rome's international airport. They were planning to shoot down an Israeli airliner. They had already set up two SAM-7s when the police burst in, acting on a tip from Mossad, the Israeli intelligence agency.

Surprisingly, there has been only one other such attempt since then. Nevertheless, international aviation authorities are uncomfortably aware of the grim possibilities of these handy, portable, simple-to-operate weapons. In the words of Captain Thomas M. Ashwood of the Airline Pilots Association, testifying before a Senate committee in 1979, the surface-to-air missile may become "the most ominous escalation in the bloody history of terrorism."

Less accurate but still widely used are portable rocket launchers for use against targets on the ground, such as tanks and other vehicles, buildings, and even personnel. Americans know these as "bazookas." Most commonly used by terrorists over the past decade has been the Soviet RPG-7. In the mid-1970s the notorious Carlos used an RPG-7 in two separate attempts to destroy Israeli airliners at Orly airport outside Paris. He missed both times.

There also exists an array of exotic weaponry that seems more appropriate to science fiction than to reality. A few drops of certain new chemical compounds, for example, can easily be sprayed, sprinkled, dripped, or otherwise conveyed onto a victim's skin. The result is paralysis and death. More fantastic is a tiny hypodermic device rigged to inject into the victim a tiny pellet filled with poison. In one widely publicized 1978 incident, Soviet agents used this weapon, built into an umbrella, to execute a recent defector to the West as he was strolling on a London street.

Another murderous refinement is the cyanide-tipped bullet. This was adopted as a sort of trademark by the Symbionese Liberation Army, the tiny underground American gang that earned worldwide notoriety by kidnapping heiress Patty Hearst in 1974. Its members drilled tiny holes in the lead tips of their bullets, filled them with deadly cyanide crystals, and sealed them with wax. The theory was that if a bullet failed to kill, the poison would.

As we shall see, the future holds even more menacing possibilities in the form of terrorist weapons vastly more potent than any discussed thus far.

V.

FROM TRAINING INTO ACTION

"We must anticipate increasing numbers of violent acts as the 1980s advance."

This frightening prediction sums up the considered judgment of a leading authority on world terrorism, Anthony C. E. Quainton, director of the U.S. State Department's Office for Combatting Terrorism. The statistics certainly bear Quainton out.

The CIA began keeping statistical records on terrorism in 1968. In a report issued in 1981, the CIA stated that there had been over 6,700 attacks worldwide by left-wing terrorists over the intervening twelve years. About 3,700 persons died, and 7,500 were wounded.

For reasons that are controversial, the CIA does not keep count of right-wing terrorist operations. The agency counts only "international terrorist attacks." It views rightist outrages as merely "domestic violence . . . difficult to categorize and analyze." *Newsweek* magazine recently pointed out in a critique of CIA record-keeping

Terrorism's Human Toll*

Killed**

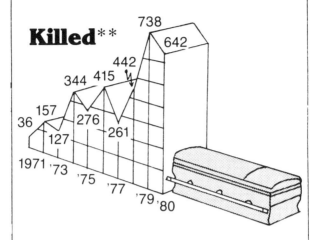

738
642
442
344 415
157
36
276
127
261
1971 '73 '75 '77 '79 '80

Injured**

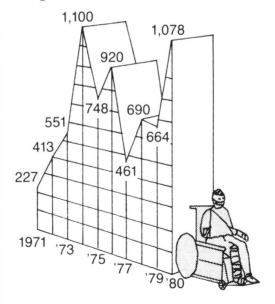

1,100
1,078
920
748 690
551
664
413
227
461
1971 '73 '75 '77 '79 '80

*Source: *Patterns of International Terrorism: 1980,* National Foreign Assessment Center, Central Intelligence Agency, 1981.

**These statistics exclude most attacks by right-wing terrorists which The CIA terms "domestic violence...difficult to categorize and analyze."

that the operations of the right had international backing at least as often as those of the left.

If right-wing attacks were included, the totals would be much higher. Startling examples can be cited from the bitter conflicts between leftists and rightists currently under way in several Central American countries. In El Salvador, for instance, in the single year 1980, the Roman Catholic Bishop's Legal Aid Commission reported about thirteen hundred persons executed by right-wing terrorist gangs known as death squads. In neighboring Guatemala, according to *The New York Times*, December 21, 1981, rightist death squads had killed three hundred people a month for the past two years. Both sides in the Central American area receive aid from abroad.

Whatever their shortcomings, the CIA statistics do show that the overall trend in international terrorist attacks is upward. The year 1980 alone accounted for 760 leftist attacks, with almost two thousand casualties.

The highest number of attacks took place in Western Europe. The Middle East and Latin America were approximately tied for second place. North America was third.

But North America, mainly the United States, had by far the highest proportion of victims. Twice as many Americans were victimized in leftist attacks, compared with Europeans or Middle Easterners, and nearly five times as many, compared with Latin Americans. United States personnel, and the facilities in which they lived and worked, were attacked in every corner of the globe.

Diplomats of all nationalities were the most common victims. There were two hundred attacks against dip-

Nationality of Victims of International Terrorist Attacks, 1968-80*

Total Incidents: 6,714

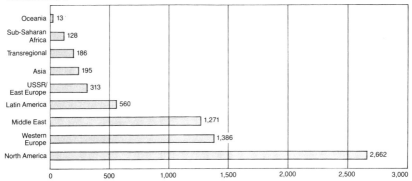

Oceania	13
Sub-Saharan Africa	128
Transregional	186
Asia	195
USSR/ East Europe	313
Latin America	560
Middle East	1,271
Western Europe	1,386
North America	2,662

0   500   1,000   1,500   2,000   2,500   3,000

*Source: *Patterns of International Terrorism: 1980,* National Foreign Assessment Center, Central Intellience Agency, 1981

Geographic Distribution of International Terrorist Attacks Directed Against U.S. Targets, 1968-80*

Total: 2,949

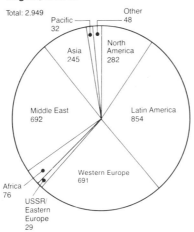

Other 48
Pacific 32
Asia 245
North America 282
Middle East 692
Latin America 854
Africa 76
USSR/ Eastern Europe 29
Western Europe 691

*Source: *Patterns of International Terrorism: 1980,* National Foreign Assessment Center, Central Intelligence Agency, 1981

Terrorist attacks against U.S. personnel and facilities*

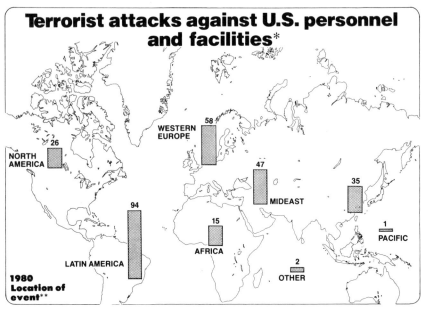

WESTERN EUROPE 58

NORTH AMERICA 26

MIDEAST 47

35

94

15
AFRICA

1
PACIFIC

2
OTHER

LATIN AMERICA

**1980
Location of event***

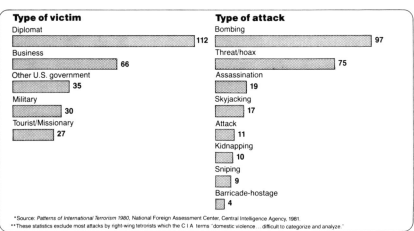

Type of victim

Diplomat
112

Business
66

Other U.S. government
35

Military
30

Tourist/Missionary
27

Type of attack

Bombing
97

Threat/hoax
75

Assassination
19

Skyjacking
17

Attack
11

Kidnapping
10

Sniping
9

Barricade-hostage
4

*Source: *Patterns of International Terrorism 1980*, National Foreign Assessment Center, Central Intelligence Agency, 1981.
**These statistics exclude most attacks by right-wing terrorists which the C I A terms "domestic violence … difficult to categorize and analyze."

lomats throughout the world in 1970; by 1981 that figure had doubled. Businessmen were the second most frequent victims, followed by other government officials, military men, tourists, and missionaries.

Shocking as the CIA figures may appear, they tell only part of the story. They exclude terrorist acts that were not international in nature.

Consider the seemingly endless strife in Northern Ireland. That one tormented country experienced more than ten thousand bombings during the 1970s. By early 1982 more than two thousand persons had died, including 346 British soldiers and 163 Irish policemen.

The situation in Italy is even grimmer. In 1979 Italy alone witnessed 2,750 terrorist operations. Credit for these was claimed by an astonishing 215 left-wing groups.

One reason for the mounting tide of terrorist attacks has been a steady increase in unemployment among the highly educated and articulate young in the world's urban centers. In this age of science and technology, society needs ever-increasing numbers of technicians, engineers, and scientists. Young people trained for careers in law, the liberal arts, and the humanities find that too often there seems to be no place for them. The inevitable result is resentment, anger, and, in all too many instances, a turn toward violence.

Still another factor has helped promote the spread of terrorism. It is the development of highly perfected organizational methods. Today's terrorist groups are set up in ways masterfully designed to frustrate intelligence and undercover operations by government agents.

The system in widest use was first developed by the

Tupamaros, the terrorist force that very nearly dragged the orderly and democratic nation of Uruguay to total chaos in the late 1960s and early 1970s. West Germany's Baader-Meinhof Gang and Italy's Red Brigades were organized along lines copied almost exactly from the Tupamaros.

There are two ways of looking at this system: the concentric-circles view, and the cell-column view.

The most visible aspect of the concentric-circles form of organization is the outer fringe of individuals who sympathize with the cause but are only occasionally active on its behalf. They can usually be counted on for financial contributions, but they never expose themselves to public criticism or suspicion. Some of these people may even be in the government, giving the terrorists good possibilities for intelligence-gathering.

More active supporters form another circle closer to the center of things but still not formally linked to the organization in any way. These people are still "legal" and respectable. They may, for instance, attend public rallies and demonstrations, but they never engage in any form of illegal behavior.

Next is the circle of "stringers." These individuals have channels of contact to the terrorist center. They are called on to obtain information and pass it to the center and to carry out specific assignments on a one-at-a-time basis. They are not permitted to know anything about strategic plans and policy.

Finally we come to the actual members of the terrorist organization. That brings us to the cell-column system.

The members are organized into small groups known as cells, not all of which are equally trusted. Some cells are regarded as useful only for relatively minor or secondary logistic missions. They might be ordered to steal vehicles needed for an operation, for example, but they would be excluded from the operation itself.

Closest to the center are cells composed of deeply indoctrinated and thoroughly committed activists. These are the battle-hardened fighters, the trained killers, the hit men of terrorism. The center itself comprises the hard core of full-time revolutionaries who determine the broad strategy and tactics for the entire organization.

A cell usually includes from two to six members. Every effort is made to ensure that these people do not know one another's true identity, although this will obviously not always be possible among people who are often friends, neighbors, or colleagues at work.

Several cells are brought together to form a column. Again measures are taken to prevent the members of any cell from knowing the members of any other cell. Only the leaders of each cell will ever actually meet. Their job is to coordinate the work of their cells. Usually the column will be responsible for a given geographical area.

All units in the organization are represented in the national convention, which is theoretically supposed to meet about every eighteen months to set broad policy. Under the conditions that generally beset such organizations, however, this national convention can rarely come together on any regular basis. In its absence, decisions are made by an executive committee of perhaps half a dozen individuals.

This type of multilayered arrangement is difficult for

law-enforcement agencies to deal with. The authorities will often succeed quite easily in identifying supporters of a terrorist movement, the kind of respectable individuals who form the outer edges of the organization. But arresting and interrogating large numbers of law-abiding people serves no real purpose. They know nothing of the group's inner workings and can supply little if any useful information.

If undercover law-enforcement agents do somehow manage to penetrate deeper, they encounter the complicated maze of columns and cells. Each of these has little connection with or knowledge about the others. Furthermore, infiltration is dangerous when cell members know one another well (though not always each other's real identities). Strangers must undergo the most grueling scrutiny before they can win acceptance.

For combat operations, many terrorist groups have adopted an organizational setup recommended by Marighella in his minimanual. Four or five persons selected for an attack are combined into a "firing group." At least one of them should be armed with an automatic weapon. The others may carry .38-caliber revolvers, their "standard arm." Hand grenades and smoke bombs round out the firing group's weaponry.

The ideal attack plan deploys two firing groups under a single commander. This constitutes a firing team.

Marighella viewed each firing group as a practically independent force capable of planning and executing its own actions. The group must, of course, stand ready at all times to take orders from superior authority within the terrorist organization, but it should not remain inactive while awaiting orders. "Any firing group,"

Marighella declared, "can decide to assault a bank, to kidnap or execute an agent of the dictatorship . . . or a North American spy."

Once the terrorists are organized for action, the next step is target selection. Targets are picked for any one of a number of purposes. The target may be purely symbolic, as in the Puerto Rican nationalists' eight-hour seizure of the Statue of Liberty in 1977. Presumably their organization, the FALN, meant to dramatize what it viewed as the contradiction between America's ideals as symbolized by the famous monument and its "colonialist oppression" of the people of Puerto Rico.

The target may be chosen for political effect rather than for its value as a symbol. An example that plunged an entire nation into mourning was the kidnapping and eventual assassination of Italy's former prime minister, Aldo Moro. He had just negotiated a compromise between the communist party and the ruling Christian Democrats. The communists were to be allowed a share of governmental power for the first time in three decades. Moro was on his way to present this proposal for approval by the Italian Parliament on the day he was seized. If approved, as was almost certain, the new arrangement would probably have stabilized the Italian political situation for some time.

But Moro never got there. Red Brigade kidnappers trapped his car on the way. They submachine-gunned his driver, his bodyguard, and three police officers in a second car. Moro endured a harrowing fifty-five-day ordeal, but in the end the government rejected the terrorists' demands. His body, ripped by eleven pointblank shots, was dumped in the luggage compartment of a small hatchback car and abandoned on a street in Rome. The only statesman big enough to put through a bold political compromise had been cut down.

Targets are frequently selected for their disruptive effect on everyday life. Blowing up a tower carrying high-tension electric power lines, thereby blacking out part of some urban center, is one such technique. The theory behind actions of this type is that a society whose normal functioning has been thoroughly upset will be an easier mark for revolutionary overthrow than one that is stable and orderly. In reality, such actions often boomerang. People who have been seriously inconvenienced are more likely to resent the bombers who caused the inconvenience than to adopt their ideas.

A bizarre example of disruptive action was the Palestinians' 1977 project which involved injecting liquid mercury into Israeli oranges intended for the international export market. The objective was to damage the Israeli economy by cutting off a major source of revenue. The probability is that relatively few oranges were injected, but the idea was highly effective for a brief period. As fear spread, the public avoided all Israeli fruit.

But the possibility that thousands of innocent persons might be poisoned turned public opinion against the Palestinians. In addition, the Israelis immediately tightened security precautions to protect their exports. The Palestinians soon abandoned the project.

It had, however, accomplished one goal that may be the most influential single factor affecting target selection: it had garnered enormous publicity for the Palestinian cause.

Publicity is the primary goal underlying almost all terrorist actions. Terrorists believe—and they have often been proven correct on this point—that their cause will almost inevitably benefit from being brought forcefully to public attention. Even when the public's original response to any particular operation is unfavorable, the result will be to raise public consciousness of the cause and eventually to ensure increased public sympathy for it.

In this sense terrorism is often described as a form of theater. Actions are intended not so much for their effect on those immediately involved, such as a group of hostages, as for their effect on the "audience" of the outside world. That audience, the terrorists believe, can be so powerfully affected through the media that it will pressure the authorities to yield to their demands.

The case of the Palestinians demonstrates how this works. Some of their anti-Zionist attacks at first caused wide public revulsion. In some instances the primary victims were children.

The most broadly publicized terrorist action of all time was the Palestinian seizure of the Israeli Olympic athletes in 1972. A worldwide audience estimated at 500 million people was transfixed in horror at the scenes shown live on their television sets during that dramatic daylong crisis. As it drew to its climax, German police sharpshooters could be glimpsed as they gunned down some of the terrorists, but missed others. These could then be seen hurling grenades into the helicopters that held nine young Israeli hostages. It was transformed instantly into a blazing inferno, incinerating them all.

The initial public response was sympathy for the victims. There was also considerable public resentment against the Palestinians for disrupting an event aimed at promoting international friendship. It was not long, however, before the general public began to develop a heightened curiosity about the cause that could have provoked such a dramatic act.

The eventual outcome was ever-widening official recognition for the Palestinians by governments around the world. The culmination came in 1974, when Yasir Arafat, head of the PLO, was invited to address the General Assembly of the United Nations. The PLO had become "respectable," and its leader had been transformed from an outlaw into a world statesman.

To ensure such desirable results, terrorists seek out targets most likely to produce the maximum in media attention. But no matter how publicity-worthy any given target may be, they will tend to avoid it if it appears strongly defended or difficult of access. In the words of George Habash, leader of the Popular Front for the Liberation of Palestine, "The main point is to select targets where success is 100 percent assured."

One famous incident produced all the publicity the terrorists could possibly have desired, but the final outcome was very much less than 100 percent success. This was the sensational 1974 kidnapping of Patty Hearst, heiress to one of America's great newspaper publishing families. She was kidnapped by a terrorist gang that called itself the Symbionese Liberation Army (SLA).

The SLA was founded in 1973 and based in the San Francisco area. Never very large, it was formed out of a decidedly strange mix of young, highly educated, middle-class whites—mostly women—and young black men with extensive prison records. They had come together through a volunteer program for the benefit of black prisoners at Vacaville Prison, near San Francisco.

Leader of the group was Donald De Freeze, an escapee from Soledad Prison. Much of his long criminal record involved the use of armed violence. De Freeze adopted the name "Cinque," after an African prince who led a successful mutiny aboard one of the slave ships bringing blacks to America in the early nineteenth century. He also assumed the exalted rank of "General Field Marshal."

The SLA claimed to be the first group genuinely intending to bring the black and white races together. Hence the name "Symbionese," from the word "symbiosis," which denotes a relationship in which both parties benefit. Actually, the SLA in its most active period had exactly two black and nine white members.

Like other underground American groups of that era, the SLA devoted some months to training and ideological indoctrination before going into action. Members devoted many days to exhaustive study and discussion of the works of Marx, Lenin, and other revolutionary leaders.

The SLA mounted its first operation in November 1973. Two of its members assassinated Marcus Foster, superintendent of schools in Oakland, across the bay from San Francisco. He was supposedly guilty of setting up a "fascist" system in the schools by insisting that all students carry ID cards.

Since Dr. Foster was a much admired and progressive educator as well as one of the few black officials to attain such an important post, the SLA's act shocked even the nation's radicals. The Black Panthers, then regarded as one of the most extreme of all civil rights groups, denounced the murder. Black radical leader Angela Davis termed the SLA "anti-revolutionary and puerile."

The SLA ignored its critics. On February 4, 1974, they kidnapped Patty Hearst, an art history student at the University of California in Berkeley. As ransom the SLA demanded that the Hearst family provide every needy person in California with $70 worth of food within thirty days. Patty was forced to tape-record several messages pleading for compliance with the SLA's demands. Somehow the family did manage to get several million dollars' worth of food distributed in record time.

Patty was still not freed. Instead, a new tape was produced in April, in which Patty announced that she had been convinced of the justice of the SLA cause. She had decided to "stay and fight." Her new comrades had even given her a new name, "Tania," after the Bolivian woman who fought and died at the side of the famous guerrilla leader, Che Guevara.

The real shocker came two weeks later. With De Freeze and the others, Patty took part in a daring San Francisco bank robbery. Bank cameras caught her in the act, wielding a semi-automatic M-1 carbine. Two persons were wounded, though not by her. The SLA got away with $11,000. The big question, disputed and discussed endlessly in all the media, was whether Patty had really acted of her own free will.

Shortly after the robbery, police recognized two SLA members, Bill and Emily Harris, in a sporting goods store in a Los Angeles suburb. Patty was waiting outside in a car. She made it possible for the Harrises to get away by firing an automatic rifle through the store window.

The police were closing in, however. They soon located the SLA headquarters, a bungalow in a run-down section of Los Angeles. Six SLA members, including De Freeze, died in the resulting shoot-out, but neither Patty nor the Harrises were there.

The trio was finally caught in San Francisco in September 1975. Patty Hearst returned to her family. She was eventually tried and convicted for her role in the bank robbery. She served almost two years in prison.

Patty Hearst's ordeal shed light on an aspect of terrorism that has been insufficiently studied: the psychological effects it has on the kidnap victims. Her suffering was so extreme that she barely survived. Her weight dropped from 107 to 87 pounds. Clumps of her hair fell out. Her IQ dropped 40 points from its original high level of 130. She experienced severe menstrual pain, probably as a consequence of the repeated rapes to which she was subjected.

Asked later how she was persuaded to cooperate with her captors, she could only say, "I snapped, I suppose. It was the only way I could hold on. Bend or die."

What did the whole SLA rampage mean? For a few months this tiny gang made itself the most publicized terrorist force in the world. Had it moved America one step closer to revolution? Had it eased any of the profound social problems it had so loudly denounced? The answer, quite obviously, is that SLA achieved absolutely nothing beyond a few glaring headlines.

From all accounts by men and women who have

known the kind of underground life Patty Hearst shared with her SLA captors, it is a terribly stressful experience. Claire Sterling, a journalist and author who has studied terrorism for many years, described it in her 1981 book *The Terror Network* as "a life of corroding anxiety and dismal drudgery." She quotes a former West German terrorist:

> An operation was always a relief. The real stress came from life in the group. You were always sitting around with the same people in the same flat, with the same personal problems that were never solved. . . . Once, we came to blows about where to go for breakfast.

Another member of the same group commented on the security obsession that haunts the underground life:

> Code, decode, memorize a new code, get the addresses in your head and burn the written notes, learn a text by heart, backtrack for hours before keeping an appointment. . . .80% of your time in clandestinity is spent on security. It's crazy.

A twenty-page Red Brigade booklet, *Security Rules and Work Methods,* outlines the strict procedures. It tries to regulate every conceivable facet of life in hiding, from renting or buying a safe house and the proper care and maintenance of automobiles to what to do in case of arrest.

According to this booklet, apartments used as safe houses will be most secure if located in working-class sections. They should be kept neat and orderly and must be fully furnished. Everything must appear normal from the outside. There should be curtains, a nameplate, house plants. Doors must be secured with special locks and should be armor-plated if possible.

Terrorists living underground must dress neatly and inconspicuously. A terrorist must develop a complete false identity and must live in a manner that fits the identity. If pretending to be a worker, for instance, the individual must leave home punctually every morning and not return until the appropriate time in the evening.

Automobiles must be regarded as "the property of the organization" and treated accordingly. They are to be kept in top running order and should be clean at all times, because dirty cars can attract unwelcome attention.

The harshest of all terrorist rules are those governing loyalty and discipline. Even minor offenses incur severe punishments. In the IRA and the Red Brigades, "kneecapping" has long been a favorite penalty. This is done by shooting the victim through the back of the knee (although the IRA has been known in especially serious cases to use an electric drill for kneecappings). In a recent ten-year period, IRA courts have ordered eight hundred of these "punishment shootings."

Crimes subject to this and other penalties can range from keeping part of the money taken in a robbery to attempting to quit active duty. For the supreme crime of active collaboration with the authorities, the penalty is invariably execution.

VI.

WHERE DOES THE MONEY COME FROM?

Terrorism is expensive.

The cost of maintaining a single full-time Red Brigade underground activist in 1980 was estimated at about $15,000 a year. The Red Brigades were then at top strength, with an estimated five hundred underground fighters. One year's ordinary expenses for all of them amounted to at least $8 million. And Italy at that time had an inflation rate of about 20 percent. Costs are much higher today.

Even these sums do not cover active operations. Transportation alone constitutes a major additional expense, with jet travel, fast cars, and a varied array of water-borne craft.

Modern communications and information equipment does not come cheaply either. Two Red Brigade safe houses near Venice were raided in 1980. One featured an extensive microfilm library containing Brigade records for a whole decade. Electronic equipment found in the other safe house included closed-circuit television equipment, a videotelex, powerful radio transmitters of the type used by law-enforcement authorities, and an impressive variety of testing and maintenance gear. The total estimated value was in excess of $250,000.

Consider the expenses incurred by a terrorist or a team of terrorists stalking some prominent man prior to kidnapping him. They must learn about his daily habits and routine, his friends, his business associates, his family, his favorite forms of recreation. If they are going to remain inconspicuous while sticking as close as possible to their quarry, the stalkers must be able to afford clothes comparable in elegance and variety to those he wears. Their cars must be as costly as his.

Life on the run has other special costs. There is a constant need for new clothing. Men and women who often have to leave their secret hideouts in a hurry cannot usually take their wardrobes with them.

A less dramatic but essential financial burden is support for the families of activists killed, wounded, or imprisoned. The larger and more stable groups maintain regular pension funds. Widows of PLO fighters were receiving $75 a month in the late 1970s; parents got $25, brothers and sisters got $10, and children got $5 each. These amounts may have been raised since then.

Success sometimes brings its own costs. The PLO has won recognition from governments around the world and from the United Nations. For the PLO this has meant having to set up and maintain offices that function almost as official embassies in nearly a hundred countries. The heads of the principal offices in Europe and North America receive salaries of between $1,500 and $2,000 a month, plus expenses. Obviously there are considerable additional costs in rents, office equipment, and staff salaries.

By way of contrast, the ordinary fighter in the PLO ranks receives $70 a month. Nor do the wretched thousands of Palestinians huddled in the squalid refugee camps receive much aid from PLO coffers. The dire poverty and unemployment in the camps ensures the PLO of a steady flow of recruits.

The costs of maintaining a sizable armed force and a far-flung organization have never been as serious a problem for the PLO as they would be for any other terrorist organization. As *Time* magazine put it, "The Palestinians have what is probably the richest, best-financed revolutionary-terrorist organization in history."

In 1979 Saudi Arabia pledged $250 million a year to the PLO. Substantial though lesser contributions were coming in from the other Arab states. The Libyan dictator Muammar Qaddafi donated regularly, but especially enjoyed giving generous bonuses to individuals who had carried out successful operations. The Soviet Union and China could be counted on for arms and other supplies.

An additional source was the approximately 300,000 Palestinians working in the Persian Gulf oil states. They were regularly taxed 5 percent of their wages for the PLO's benefit. The levy amassed $10 million annually. Wealthy Palestinians living in the West also chipped in considerable amounts.

PLO assets in 1979 included an investment portfolio estimated at above $100 million. Among its holdings abroad are hotels, shipyards, oil tankers, and television stations. Its financial reach has penetrated major U.S. companies operating in the Middle East.

A large part of this wealth is managed through the Arab Bank Ltd., a $4-billion institution based in Amman, Jordan, but controlled by Palestinians. Well known throughout the Middle East as "the PLO bank," it has branches or a share in varied enterprises in nearly two dozen countries, including the United States.

This impressive array of financial power was hit hard by the 1982 Israeli blitz in Lebanon. The PLO's principal bases, training camps, and most of its huge arms depots were either captured or destroyed. A large part of its guerrilla force was driven out of the country. PLO leaders were shocked to find the formerly supportive Arab world suddenly aloof and indifferent. PLO finances, especially its former sources of income, were imperiled.

No other terrorist organization has ever come even remotely close to the PLO in the days of its greatest affluence. Most have to resort to more violent measures to get the funds they need.

Bank-robbing has long been a favored technique. The Baader-Meinhof Gang was so successful at it that for a time the German banks were popularly known as "terrorist treasuries." Ulrike Meinhof, founder of the gang, pronounced bank-robbing "tactically correct because it is a proletarian action" and "strategically correct because it serves the financing of the guerrilla." It is swift, the results are often hugely enriching, and at the same time it seems a direct blow at one of capitalism's most basic institutions.

Marighella recommended this method highly in his minimanual: "We have almost made [bank-robbing] a kind of entrance exam for apprenticeship in the technique of revolutionary war." He warned, however, that terrorists must be considerate of ordinary people who might happen to be in a bank during a robbery. Their money should not be taken, and they should not be hurt in any way. Otherwise they might become confused about the lofty revolutionary purpose behind the robbery.

Some groups have favored kidnapping for ransom. As one example, Argentina's ERP was able to accumulate a war chest of $30 million in the mid-1970s through a series of kidnappings of executives of big multinational corporations. Members of ERP justified this method as "a correct radical approach" on the grounds that seizing foreign officials of foreign-owned businesses would help rid their country of "imperialist" influences.

Some of the ransoms the Argentine kidnappers collected were of mind-boggling size. For the safe release of one Exxon executive, ERP got $14 million. The group topped this in 1975 by getting $60 million in cash, plus a distribution of $1.2 million in food and clothing to the poor, for the return of the two sons of one of the country's most important big-business magnates.

Other groups have even resorted to acting as mercenaries in return for financial assistance. The Japanese Red Army, for instance, has been almost totally dependent on the Popular Front for the Liberation of Palestine since being driven out of its own country in the early 1970s. The group's 1972 attack on a waiting room full of airline passengers in Israel signaled the beginning of this terrorism-for-hire. West German terrorists, too, are known to have received Arab money in payment for operations against Israeli and other Jewish targets in Germany.

The Red Brigades have also experienced occasional difficulty in meeting their yearly budget requirement of approximately $10 million. One solution has been to form a partnership with organized crime. Bank robberies, kidnappings, and other forms of extortion are types of operations that the terrorists can easily and almost naturally share with Italy's professional criminals.

At the same time, the Red Brigades have managed to invest substantial sums. Brigade funds were especially considerable in real estate, a long-term form of investment indicating that the Brigades expected to be in business for some time. Like the Palestinians, the Red Brigades also have maintained a regular pension system for those either killed or captured.

The IRA's financial story is quite different. Until recently, Irish Americans were its biggest source of support. They contributed mainly through the Irish North American Aid Committee. But collections from the United States began to decline in the mid-1970s. The reasons reveal much about the politics of terrorism.

For many years IRA fund-raisers in the United States had been under strict orders to avoid all public references to the organization's ultimate goal of a socialist Ireland. They were also to remain silent about the IRA's long-standing conflicts with the Catholic church. The respectable, hard-working, God-fearing Irish Americans who were the IRA's fiscal mainstay could only be repelled by knowledge of such unpleasant realities.

Instead, IRA speakers were instructed to emphasize themes sure to evoke positive sentiments. They should remind their listeners of the devastating potato famine of the middle and late 1840s, which forced the ancestors of today's Irish Americans to emigrate to America in great numbers. They should revive the glorious memories of the Troubles—the great Easter Rebellion of 1916 and the no-quarter-asked guerrilla war against the British Black and Tans in 1920–22. The IRA's many celebrated martyrs were to be memorialized at every opportunity. Fund-raisers were to exploit anti-British feeling to the maximum. The IRA's goal was to be described as a free and united Ireland—nothing more.

The IRA's propaganda in the United States has been undermined in recent years by a sustained counter-campaign by the Irish government. Certain well-known Irish Americans, most notably Senator Edward Kennedy of Massachusetts and Speaker of the U.S. House of Representatives Thomas J. O'Neill, have also spoken out against IRA extremism. United States Ambassador to Ireland William V. Shannon summed up the situation by noting that Irish Americans have grown newly aware of the "realities and complexities of the situation in the North."

The resulting drop in funding from the United States has compelled the IRA to seek other sources. Bank robberies have increased tremendously in frequency in both parts of Ireland. In one recent year the Provos took an estimated £2 million ($4 million) in an astonishing 215 bank heists.

Once almost all IRA weapons were American. Today they are increasingly of Soviet manufacture, supplied through Libya, the Palestinians, and the Soviet satellites in Eastern Europe.

Inevitably, so drastic a shift in its sources of support has brought other basic changes in IRA policy. The group formerly kept itself relatively aloof from the international terrorist network. Nowadays the IRA is increasingly drawn into international and transnational operations. Small groups of IRA recruits are known to have trained in Middle Eastern camps in recent years. A few terrorists from other countries have come to Northern Ireland to observe and sometimes even to participate in IRA operations.

In some ways, terrorism in the United States has undergone a development similar to that of the IRA. In the heyday of American radical extremism in the late 1960s and early 1970s, sizable sums could often be raised in open and above-board ways. Large sections of the public actively sympathized with the two central causes of that era, the crusade for civil rights and the anti–Vietnam War movement. As these grew in public appeal, so did financial contributions. Popular stars of the entertainment world often performed and spoke in behalf of these causes, bringing in big amounts at rallies and benefit appearances.

The organizations aided by these activities were by and large legitimate, nonviolent, reform groups. They were seeking to rectify what they viewed as genuine grievances. It is possible that some portion of the funds collected was siphoned off for underground extremists. What is certain is that substantial sums of money were being gathered for the underground at the same time, but in less open ways.

This secret fund-raising is evidenced by the fact that a

number of well-known radicals went into hiding during those years. Actively pursued by both federal and local authorities, some evaded capture for nearly a decade. They could hardly have done so without generous support from their covert sympathizers, in the form of safe havens, message drops, and money.

Extralegal fund-raising methods were of course also employed. Aping the terrorists of that era in other countries, the American militants resorted to bank robbery, kidnapping, and extortion.

Relentless pressure from the authorities brought about a shrinkage of the ultra-leftist forces within the United States in the late 1970s and early 1980s. Many underground leaders came out of hiding and simply gave themselves up. The botched attempt to rob the Brink's armored car in Nanuet, New York, in October 1981 may have been the ultra-left's last desperate grab for a financial stake.

Terrorism is not quite dead in the United States, however. According to the FBI, the most active terrorist groups here are the Puerto Rican nationalist FALN and certain anti-Castro Cuban organizations. Sources of funding for the FALN are under constant, intense investigation. The Cuban groups derive most of their money from the 750,000 mostly middle-class Cubans now in the United States. As we have seen, some of the Cuban forces have received U.S. Government backing. The extent to which such backing continues today is impossible to determine with any degree of precision; this is classified information.

Also active within the United States are the extreme right-wing American groups. These include two organizations in direct, sometimes violent conflict with each other: the American Nazi Party and the Jewish Defense League. Much larger and more dangerous than either of these is the Ku Klux Klan.

The Klan's racist and anti-democratic activities have attracted growing numbers of followers in recent years. Its influence in some parts of the country has swelled markedly. A recent shoot-out on the streets of Greensboro, North Carolina, in which four leftist demonstrators were killed and several others wounded, went unpunished even though news film showed the killers in action.

For many years, there was no one Ku Klux Klan. Four major groups claimed the title, and there were several lesser ones. They all preached the same doctrines of hatred and violence, and they occasionally collaborated. But they seemed to compete for the same funding sources, which were believed to consist principally of private individuals. In September 1982 it was reported that rival Klans involving 80 percent of Klan membership had merged into a new confederation of Klans. Current evidence indicates that the group's finances are as yet limited, but they are growing. A dire threat to American democracy grows with them.

No expert has yet succeeded in putting together a reliable estimate of the total financing available to terrorists worldwide. The figure would unquestionably amount to hundreds of millions of dollars. It would constitute an awesome indicator of world instability.

On the one hand, there seems to be reason for optimism. As has been shown, some of the principal terrorist organizations—the PLO, the IRA, the Red

Brigades, the Latin American and United States groups—have all suffered recent setbacks. Their fund-raising capabilities have been gravely impaired. Their ability to launch operations on the scale of the recent past seems likely to decline as well.

Right-wing terror, on the other hand, appears to be in a phase of growth. From America's Ku Klux Klan to Central America's death squads to Europe's neo-Nazis and neo-fascists, funding is on the rise. The future re-mains troubled.

VII.

THE MIND OF THE TERRORIST

We must above all keep our hatred alive . . . hate that can push a human being beyond his natural limits and make him a cold, violent, selective, and effective killing-machine —Che Guevara.

Thus, shortly before his death, wrote the man who helped Fidel Castro come to power in Cuba and who died trying to spread the revolution to the South American continent. Few revolutionaries have been more admired, more studied, more imitated by today's terrorists.

Many who enter the terrorist life deliberately strive to carry out Che Guevara's advice. The more dedicated they are to the cause, the more selfless and idealistic their nature, the harder they struggle to reach beyond their "natural limits." Their efforts are aided by the extreme measures taken in the training camps to strip young recruits of normal human affections and transform them into cold-blooded "killing-machines."

But the human personality is variable, complex, often unpredictable. Different individuals react to the same stimuli in unexpected ways. The extent to which any

91

man or woman can be as profoundly steeped in hatred
as Che Guevara urged depends on what kind of person
he or she was before enlisting.

Who, then, are the terrorists? What kinds of human
beings choose to abandon normal life for the arduous
career of the outlaw?

The experts agree on at least one point. There is no
such thing as a typical terrorist. They are about as varied
in their personalities as any group of their age and social
standing. A 1979 Rand Corporation survey showed that
the revolutionaries as a group did not stand out as being
unusually heroic or especially brilliant or of a particularly saintly disposition.

Certain general characteristics, however, are shared
by most of them. In 1977 Charles A. Russell and Bow-
man H. Miller did an extensive study of terrorist traits.
It was published as "Profile of a Terrorist." Russell and
Miller gathered data on 340 activists from many countries. The subjects belonged to eighteen different urban
gangs.

Most were young. The average age in most groups
was between twenty-two and twenty-five. The West
Germans, Japanese, and Palestinians averaged a little
older: twenty-eight to thirty-one. Oldest of all were the
men and women of the IRA, which has been in action
longer than any other terrorist organization. But by the
late 1970s a tendency was developing in certain groups
(the Basques, Irish, Iranians, and Turks) to recruit
younger people, including teenagers. This may have
been a result of losses among the older cadres, stem-
ming from successful counterterrorist campaigns.

A PLO recruiting document captured in July 1982
included this statement: "Those under twelve years of

age will not be accepted." The obvious implication is that the PLO was enlisting recruits twelve years and older.

The leaders tend to be older. Yasir Arafat of the PLO and George Habash of the PFLP are in or near their fifties. Renato Curcio, founder of the Red Brigades, was thirty-five at the time of his arrest in 1976. That was the year when Ulrike Meinhof of West Germany committed suicide in prison; she was forty-two.

More than 80 percent of all terrorists are men. Women tend to serve mainly in support roles. They are expected to help gather intelligence information, to act as couriers and nurses, to maintain the safe houses.

The German groups and some American bands such as the Weather Underground are exceptions in this respect. In these groups women make up a much higher percentage than elsewhere, and they participate fully in all operations.

There have been a few outstanding women leaders: Gudrun Ensselin and Ulrike Meinhof of the Baader-Meinhof Gang, Leila Khaled of the PFLP, Fusako Shigenobu of the Japanese Red Army, Margherita Cagal of the Red Brigades, Bernadine Dohrn and Kathy Boudin of the Weather Underground.

Three out of four terrorists are unmarried. This gives them greater mobility and flexibility. People who do not have to concern themselves about their spouses or children can devote themselves more totally to the cause, take greater risks, display bolder initiative. Single people are also better security risks, since they have no families who can be threatened if they do not cooperate with the authorities.

A majority of terrorists are from the urban middle

class and in some instances the upper class. They are usually better educated than the average citizen. Their parents are often employed in the professions as lawyers, doctors, engineers, professors. In almost all cases the parents were politically liberal or even radical, shared their children's views, and sometimes actually reared their children in a tradition of political radicalism.

An intriguing psychological factor comes into play in this connection. Well-to-do young people are often attracted to political radicalism out of a profound sense of guilt. During their student years, they become aware of the poverty, hunger, and misery that scar the lives of the majority of humanity. For some, the contrast with their own comfortable lives—which they have as yet done little to earn—becomes unbearable. They turn against the very society of which they are the most favored beneficiaries.

The process has been vividly described by Lucinda Franks in her *New York Times Magazine* study of the Weather Underground. As she saw it, these young white radicals

> traveled down a long spiral: from idealistic students to peaceful protesters to rioters trashing the street to revolutionary cadres bent on shedding their "white-skin privilege" to fugitives planting bombs in empty buildings to women and men accused of assassinating the very "people" they said they were fighting for.

Kathy Boudin, one of the Weather People captured after the bungled robbery of the Brink's armored car in Nanuet, is a noteworthy example. Her first encounter with the authorities came in her junior year at fashionable Bryn Mawr College, when she participated in a demonstration against conditions at a local black school. Many of her fellow students, totally wrapped up in their own lives and careers, could not understand such behavior. Kathy hinted at her future course of action in an article in the college paper: "If desired ends cannot be achieved within the law . . . then new methods must be adopted."

Her father, Leonard Boudin, is a prominent attorney noted for his defense of many persons jailed for radical activities. His best efforts have not always been enough to keep these people out of prison. Kathy Boudin apparently came to feel that the American system of justice was stacked against radicals: "she had to find a more powerful and forbidden way to fight injustice."

A more extreme example is the case of Suzanne Albrecht. This young West German girl was the goddaughter of one of her country's richest and most powerful men, Jurgen Ponto, chairman of the Dresden Bank. By her own admission, she had experienced nothing but kindness and generosity from him.

Ponto was selected as a terrorist target. He was closely guarded and difficult to approach. Albrecht deliberately admitted the militants to Ponto's house, knowing they planned to kill him. When she was questioned afterward, her only explanation was that she was "sick of eating caviar."

One big exception to the middle- and upper-class origin of most terrorists is the IRA. Since Roman Catholics in Northern Ireland suffer from severe discrimination in employment, they are almost all of the working class. IRA fighters differ from most other terrorists in another respect as well. Where the majority of terrorists have either had some university training or are graduate or even postgraduate students, IRA men and women tend to have quit school at an earlier age.

The lower ranks of the PLO also include substantial numbers of poor people. Many have been homeless refugees for over three decades. PLO leaders are almost all from the middle and upper class.

Russell and Miller found one recent trend of potentially ominous significance. Increasing numbers of young activists have had formal training in the skilled trades. Their capabilities as electricians, gunsmiths, mechanics, printers, and specialists in related fields make them uniquely useful for terrorist purposes.

Some psychologists claim that a large percentage of young terrorists have never been able to deal with certain personal and political experiences. These individuals start from a commitment to the highest ideals, like many of their peers. They then experience the disillusioning contrast between ideals and grim political reality. Where the well-adjusted and mature person will seek and find realistic ways of coping with the frustrations of the real world, the immature individual will seek immediate satisfaction through violent rebellion. Such individuals have difficulty adjusting to authority of any kind, whether in the form of parents or government.

Some young people, as is well known, seek alternative ways to ease these stresses. Drugs, alcohol, and sex have been favored outlets. But for others, the preferred cure for their individual problems is violent action aimed at the overthrow of hated authority. This pattern supposedly is characteristic of young terrorists.

This theory has been seriously challenged on a number of grounds. Some specialists point out that there is little reliable evidence to support the notion that most terrorists are psychologically disturbed individuals, incapable of adjusting to life's problems. The careful, detailed planning and well-timed execution that have characterized many terrorist operations are hardly typical of immature minds.

The only psychological rule that seems valid for most terrorists is the obvious one: they are extremely alienated from society. Being alienated does not necessarily mean being mentally ill.

Furthermore, attempts to explain terrorism in purely psychological terms ignore the very real political, social, and economic factors that have always motivated radical activists. Whatever the state of any extremist's psyche, whether the individual is entirely rational and realistic or not, the phenomenon of terrorism as a whole must be understood in terms of society's grave problems as well as the narrower personal ones.

Other observers have been troubled by a very different attitude that has recently appeared among some terrorists. The new tendency was described to a delegation of U.S. congressmen who met with representatives of the West German government in December 1980. The German officials said that terrorists in their country had entered a new phase about 1977. The shift coincided with the conviction of the Baader-Meinhof Gang's original leaders, who were sentenced to long prison terms. The new leaders seemed to be moving "away from political objectives and toward increasingly brutal individual actions."

An early manifestation of the new attitude was the

April 1977 murder of the German federal government's top prosecutor, Siegfried Buback: "From a motorcycle driving close up to his car, Buback and his bodyguards were killed by machine-gun fire." No political or ideological demands were even presented. It was simply an act of cold-blooded revenge, to punish Buback for prosecuting the terrorists' comrades.

Another blatant example was the shooting of Fulvio Croce, president of the Turin Lawyers Association, in broad daylight on the streets of Turin in the spring of 1977. Croce was the court-appointed defense attorney for fifty-three accused Red Brigade members. His murder had an intimidating effect. Five days later, the judge had to announce a postponement of the trial because not enough jurors were willing to serve and most of the witnesses had called in sick.

Since then there have been numerous similar attacks in both West Germany and Italy. Prosecutors, judges, and court-appointed defense lawyers have been shot down. The sole motive for these coolly calculated killings was to intimidate the authorities into delaying or even calling off the trials of captured terrorists. Such actions could have no lasting political results favorable to the revolutionary cause. They could only shock and anger the ordinary citizen, losing the terrorists whatever public sympathy they might once have enjoyed.

In 1982, at another big Red Brigade trial in Rome, a dramatic change in public attitude was evident. The terrorists' facade of invincibility and immunity from prosecution had been broken by sweeping manhunts that had netted hundreds of militants. Many had turned state's evidence. The new trial proceeded without delay or interruption. The accused were convicted and sentenced to long prison terms.

A pertinent comment was added by President Sandro Pertini of Italy during his visit to the United States in April 1982. By that time many captured Red Brigade members, including some of the organization's top leaders, had talked. Their information enabled the government to arrest many others and locate several Brigade headquarters, safe houses, and arms caches.

Pertini contrasted this behavior with that of the thousands of anti-fascists who had spent years in prisons and concentration camps under the brutal dictatorship of Mussolini and his fascist followers. Pertini himself, a much admired hero of the anti-fascist resistance, had spent fifteen years in jail. Few of the prisoners in those years, Pertini said, ever talked, although they were subjected to horrible forms of torture. The members of the Red Brigades suffered no such ordeal.

Pertini explained the difference by pointing out that the anti-fascists were people with genuine, deep-rooted political convictions. The Red Brigades had obviously lost any real political beliefs they might once have had. They cared only about saving themselves.

The most celebrated terrorist of them all, Carlos the Jackal, is a spectacular example of this self-serving attitude. In his case it is mixed with a special brand of arrogance.

Carlos's history is unique. His father, a wealthy Venezuelan real estate broker, was also a convinced communist. He had named his three sons Vladimir, Ilich, and Lenin, after the famous Bolshevik leader. The middle son, Ilich, later became Carlos.

According to a 1979 interview (the only one Carlos has ever given), he joined the Venezuelan communist party at the age of fifteen. Within a few years he headed an underground cell of two hundred members.

In 1966 he spent several months at a training camp in Cuba run by a Soviet KGB colonel. There Carlos received his grounding in terrorist weaponry, strategy, and tactics. Two years later the party sent him to Moscow. There he attended Patrice Lumumba University, a KGB institution designed to indoctrinate Third World students in the Soviet version of Marxist-Leninist theory and practice.

Carlos, who already had a considerable reputation as a playboy, misbehaved so badly in Moscow that he was expelled from the university as a "public disgrace." He went to Jordan, where he trained and fought alongside the PFLP. By 1973 he was in London. He'd made up a list of some five hundred persons, mostly Jews, to be shot.

Heading the list was Joseph Edward "Teddy" Sief, owner of a chain of clothing stores and a leading Zionist. On December 31, 1973, Carlos attempted his first assassination. He fired at Sief three times, at point-blank range. Somehow he missed with two of the three shots; the third struck Sief but was deflected by his teeth. Carlos claimed his revolver was old and defective—a dubious story for a man who had an unlimited choice of weapons. The most likely explanation is that he was drunk.

Bungling what should have been an easy killing could not stop a man with Carlos's self-assurance. Within a few months he had been chosen to head the international terrorist headquarters in Paris. He subsequently planned and organized a series of successful operations throughout Western Europe.

His deputy was a Palestinian Arab named Michel Moukharbel, who had secretly become a police informer. In June 1975 he led three police officers to Carlos's apartment in Paris. Carlos killed two of the officers and wounded the third. Then, in his own words:

> There was only Michel left in the room. He came towards me with his hands over his eyes. He knew the rules of the game: a traitor is condemned to die. He stood before me, I shot into his eyes, he fell to the ground. I shot once more into his temple. I was calm . . . walked away as if nothing had happened.

Carlos's most sensational operation was the 1975 raid on the meeting of OPEC ministers in Vienna. It was also his most lucrative, netting him a $5 million share of the $25 million ransom plus a $2 million bonus and a luxurious Libyan villa, given by dictator Qaddafi.

This operation also displayed the mindless brutality that was beginning to mark terrorist behavior. Three elderly Austrian guards were killed unnecessarily during the raid. They had put up little or no resistance. Carlos himself pumped seven slugs into one of them. Gabriele Kröcher-Tiedemann, a West German woman on the hit team, coolly shot one guard through the back of the neck as he tried to flee. Another member of the gang, Hans-Joachim Klein, was so sickened by what he called these "gangster killings" that he quit the organization immediately afterward.

During the long flight that carried the eleven kidnapped OPEC ministers to Algeria, Sheikh Zaki Yamani of Saudi Arabia had a long conversation with Carlos and observed him closely. Carlos was dressed in a manner mimicking the much publicized style of his hero, Che Guevara: trench coat, beret, beard. He was armed with a submachine gun and a Soviet Makarov automatic pistol.

Yamani concluded that Carlos was a man without genuine political convictions. He was neither a fully committed communist nor a believer in the Palestinian cause that was supposedly the motive for the entire operation.

Carlos then "retired" for several years, disappearing completely from public notice despite an international police dragnet spread over three continents. He was presumably enjoying his ill-gotten gains. This was hardly the behavior of a politically dedicated person.

He reappeared unexpectedly in March 1982. The French minister of the interior received a letter threatening a new campaign of terror unless the government of France freed two of Carlos's comrades then awaiting trial. The signature and a thumbprint carefully placed on the letter were officially confirmed as belonging to Carlos. With characteristic bravado, Carlos pledged "personally to attack the French government" unless the imprisoned pair was provided with a plane "to fly to a destination of their choice."

The French authorities refused. The two prisoners, a young Swiss man and a West German woman, were sentenced to long prison terms. It is not clear why they were of such importance to Carlos.

In the ensuing months there was a series of assassinations, both inside France and against French diplomats in Lebanon. The murders were thought to be very much "in the style of Carlos." He was also a prime suspect in the bombing of the Paris–Toulouse express train, which killed five and injured twenty-seven. But the mystery only deepened as no further word came from him. No one could be sure who the real perpetrator was. Still, an entire nation was kept in a state of raw alert because of one man.

Grandiose as Carlos's pretensions may be, they pale beside those of Muammar Qaddafi, dictator of Libya. Qaddafi has played a strange but significant role in the development of world terrorism.

In 1969 he won control of the oil-rich desert kingdom, with its vast territory and relatively tiny population of about two million. Then a young army officer, Qaddafi headed a revolt that overthrew the aged king. Qaddafi is an extremely devout Muslim and has imposed the strictest religious orthodoxy on the country.

His behavior since then has marked him as the most unpredictable leader now on the world scene. He has, for example, provided funding for both right-wing and left-wing terrorists.

For some years Qaddafi was the main financial support of the Italy-Libya Association. On the surface it appeared a normal organization for the promotion of international friendship. Actually it was a thinly veiled front for neo-fascist agitation. It was recently outlawed as such in Italy. The head of the association was one Claudio Mutti, a notorious neo-Nazi who was jailed in 1980 on suspicion of having taken part in the bombing that year of the Bologna railroad station.

At the same time, Qaddafi funds and weaponry were bolstering groups at the opposite end of the political spectrum: the PFLP, the Baader-Meinhof Gang, the Basque ETA, the IRA, and many others. There is no simple explanation for this apparent political confusion.

As far as can be determined from his public statements, Qaddafi favors some sort of "world revolution" against "imperialism," which is to be replaced by some vague form of "socialism." Yet the form of government he has set up in his own country can scarcely be distinguished from any right-wing military dictatorship.

Libya under Qaddafi's rule has become the site of the world's largest network of terrorist training camps. Out of these centers have come thousands of ultra-rightist and ultra-leftist activists, who have used Qaddafi arms and Qaddafi money to strike terror into every part of the world. He is believed to have set aside a fund totaling $1 billion a year for these purposes.

Some observers speculate that Qaddafi's specific objective is to destabilize the Middle East. His own power and prestige would presumably be enhanced as neighboring governments were undermined.

Qaddafi is known to have put up a long-standing reward of $1 million for the assassination of Egypt's Anwar Sadat. Four unsuccessful attempts resulted. But when Sadat was finally assassinated in 1981, the killers were apparently not linked to Qaddafi. Sadat, incidentally, referred to Qaddafi as "a vicious criminal, 100 percent sick and possessed of a demon."

The presidents of Niger, the Sudan, and Tunisia have all stated that Qaddafi has tried to have them put to death. Such behavior is not exactly customary for anyone claiming to be the head of a legitimate government, especially one who aspires to the rank of world statesman.

Qaddafi has been absolutely clear and unswerving about one goal: the destruction of Israel. The more extreme factions among the Palestinian terrorists have long been particular favorites of his. Anti-Israeli operations financed and/or equipped by him include the 1972 abduction of the Israeli athletes at the Munich Olympics, the 1973 plot to shoot down an Israeli airliner during takeoff from the Rome airport, Carlos's two failed attempts to blow up Israeli airliners at a Paris airport in 1975, and innumerable other actions both inside and outside Israel. His explicit instructions to one Palestinian team about to embark on one such raid: "Kill as many Jews as you can."

U.S. citizens, too, have become Qaddafi's targets. In August 1976 a young legislative aide on the staff of Senator Jacob Javits was murdered by a bomb in Istanbul. Javits later reported to a Senate subcommittee on the ensuing investigation: "The trail seems very clearly to go back to Libya, where these assassins were armed and instructed and got false passports."

Thereafter, U.S.–Libyan relations deteriorated rapidly. In December 1979 Qaddafi's police stood by while a screaming mob sacked and burned the U.S. embassy in Tripoli. This was Qaddafi's way of expressing his support for Iran's Ayatollah Khomeini, who was then holding fifty-two Americans hostage.

The United States retaliated the following spring, when President Carter ordered four Libyan diplomats expelled from this country. The diplomats threatened

Libyan students in the United States who were opposed to the Qaddafi regime. At least fifteen young Libyan dissidents have been murdered in Europe. President Ronald Reagan finally ordered the Libyan embassy in Washington closed and all Libyan diplomats expelled in May 1981.

But the most sensational anti-American plot came later that year, with Qaddafi's alleged dispatch of several hit teams to assassinate President Reagan and other top U.S. officials. According to the CIA, this was to be his revenge for the shooting down of two Libyan jets by U.S. fighters off the coast of Libya in August 1981.

Qaddafi heatedly denied it, insisting that President Reagan was "silly" and "ignorant" to believe such a thing. Evidence for the plot was contained in a forty-page National Security Council report. Security precautions for the protection of Reagan and other menaced Americans were intensified, and a nationwide manhunt was launched for the presumed Qaddafi agents. Ultimately there were no assassination attempts, possibly because the preventive measures had been successful.

In the summer of 1982 several thousand PLO fighters were trapped in West Beirut and undergoing constant bombardment by Israeli planes and artillery. Qaddafi offered a suggestion. The PLO men should all commit suicide, he announced, in order to shame the Israelis. There was no public reply from the sorely beset guerrillas.

In the confusing and contradictory tangle of Qaddafi's words and actions, it is difficult to discern any clear political viewpoint. His only consistent mental attitude is a primitive urge to assert himself as some sort of major figure in world politics.

The mind-set of today's burgeoning right-wing terrorist movement is equally simplistic. Until recently, the popular tendency was to dismiss the swaggering, strutting, uniformed neo-Nazis, neo-fascists, and Ku Klux Klansmen as a lunatic fringe that posed no serious threat to democratic societies. Their nostalgic desire to restore the "good old days," such as those the ultra-right enjoyed under Hitler and Mussolini, was regarded as unlikely to attract much support. The rightists' indiscriminate bombings and street violence of recent years and their swelling numbers have brought on second thoughts.

These groups hold a special attraction for young toughs who seek and enjoy physical violence. They are a particular problem in Spain. A newly active assortment of Spanish pro-fascist groups is agitating to restore the conditions of the recently overthrown Franco dictatorship. According to a member of the Spanish senate, the fascist youth gangs, "armed with iron bars, chains, knives, and pistols," have terrorized many cities and towns. They have been "threatening and beating the inhabitants, slashing tires, and smashing store windows."

A number of camps exist in Spain where young fascists undergo training. Some of these are headed by Germans, including at least one notorious former SS officer.

The barbarous attitude their training is designed to produce was exposed by a recent incident. In a Madrid park, ten young men from one of the camps attacked a young couple whose behavior they apparently regarded as unacceptable. Wielding a baseball bat on which the slogan "Long live fascism" had been engraved, they smashed the man's head. In one year, 1980, twenty-one

Armed Palestinian guerrillas encircling a skyjacked TWA jetliner at an airstrip near Amman, Jordan, in September 1970. The plane, one of three at that airstrip, was eventually blown up after the 180 passengers were released.

The blazing remains of the Pan Am jetliner in Cairo—one of the four skyjacked by the Popular Front for the Liberation of Palestine—after it was blown up by the guerrillas.

A Palestinian terrorist on the balcony of an Olympic village building in Munich in 1972. The terrorists held Israeli team members
hostage in the building while West German police took up positions
around the outside.

Caught by the bank camera, Patty Hearst during the 1974 robbery of a San Francisco bank by the SLA terrorist group.

The scene of the kidnapping of former Prime Minister Aldo Moro in Rome in 1978. Moro's car is the dark one in the center, behind it the bullet-riddled white escort car. In the foreground is the body of one of the five bodyguards killed in the attack.

A hooded member of the Provisional IRA waves a submachine gun during a British-troops-out rally in Belfast, Northern Ireland.

people were tortured and murdered by Spanish fascist militants.

The extreme right-wing point of view holds that the common people have been hopelessly corrupted by democracy and the welfare state. The people can be saved only by a truly great leader, who will one day take total power at the head of his pitiless, savagely loyal storm troopers. The people's role will then be a simple one: to obey.

Today there are plenty of candidates for this leadership role. They are to be found strutting and posing and shouting their rabble-rousing speeches in many parts of Western Europe and the United States.

A disturbing aspect of the current resurgence of rightist activism is the mounting evidence of involvement by military and police officers. In France the head of an independent police union revealed in late 1980 that at least thirty top French neo-Nazis were members of the police force. Some held high police rank and used their influence to hamper and delay investigations of right-wing crimes.

Similar charges have been made about the Italian law-enforcement authorities. In February 1982 a major and a former captain in the paramilitary carabinieri were arrested and formally charged with aiding neofascist terrorists. At the same time two lieutenant colonels were under investigation. The influence such high-ranking officers can wield is shown by the fact that of 150 prosecutions against ultra-rightists in Milan in a recent year, only two led to convictions. The prosecution and conviction rate for left-wing militants is much higher.

A 1981 incident in Brazil was even more embarrassing for the authorities. A bomb being carried in a sports car exploded prematurely. The car was in a parking lot just outside a crowded public auditorium. An army sergeant had been holding the bomb in his lap; he was killed instantly. A captain sitting beside him was badly wounded.

This accident led to what *The New York Times* on July 17, 1982, called "the most broad-based cover-up operation of recent times." The right-wing military dictatorship that has ruled Brazil since 1964 was desperately eager somehow to shift blame for the bungled bombing to the left-wing opposition. The cover-up failed.

About forty unsolved terrorist bombings had occurred in Brazil during the preceding sixteen months. The government-controlled media had consistently blamed them on leftists. A large part of the public remained suspicious. The almost ludicrous new incident confirmed the widespread belief that the real bombers were members of the armed forces, not the political opposition.

Clear psychological motives exist for the close link between the ultra-right and the uniformed forces of law and order. The rightist mentality feels most at home in a rigid, orderly, authoritarian system where everyone knows his or her place and obeys superior authority without question. The "correct" attitude is embodied in the slogan of Nazi Germany: "Führer commands; we obey!"

The similarity between this attitude and that of individuals most likely to feel at home in the military or the police is obvious. This does not mean that all or even most military and police officers are potential neo-Nazis. But the history of Nazi and fascist takeovers of governments does show that they have almost invariably had the active support of the armed forces. A typical instance occurred in Spain in February 1981, when a group of generals attempted to overthrow the government and restore fascism.

Both extremes within the embattled arena of terrorism have long histories. A glance into their yesterdays will help us to understand the terrorism of today—and tomorrow.

VIII.

FLASHBACK: ONE HUNDRED YEARS OF TERRORISM

Terrorism is not new. People have been assassinated, kidnapped, and held hostage many times and in many places over the centuries. Motives, methods, and outcomes have been as varied as human hopes and fears.

Modern forms of terrorism differ from earlier types in that radicals have developed more organized and systematic methods. Relatively small groups of plotters have been able to plunge whole nations into chaos by campaigns of a scope and duration never known before.

This development is well illustrated by events in five countries: Russia, Ireland, Palestine (to be viewed from both the Jewish and Palestinian sides), Uruguay, and the United States.

1. The Russians

The terroristic revolution is the only just form of revolution— Nikolai Morozov (1880).

Modern political terrorism was born in Europe's most

117

autocratic and repressive society, czarist Russia. Here the great mass of the people lived in unmatched poverty and ignorance. Peaceable attempts to loosen the stranglehold of the aristocratic ruling class met only brutal suppression. A vast secret-police network thwarted all efforts to organize the people into a democratic movement for change.

Revolutionaries like Nikolai Morozov, quoted above, could see no other way but terrorism. Slowly and cautiously at first, they formed secret organizations in several Russian cities, preparing for action. One of the earliest was set up in 1878, calling itself "The People's Will." It launched a campaign of assassinations that removed several of the nation's most prominent leaders.

Then, in 1881, the terrorists achieved what they regarded as the ultimate objective. A bomb hurled into a royal carriage in the capital, St. Petersburg, slew none other than the czar of all the Russias himself, Alexander II.

At least two political ironies are connected with the assassination of Alexander II. First, he had consciously tried to be a comparatively kindly ruler. In 1861, for example, he took the extraordinary step of emancipating the serfs, ending centuries of virtual slavery throughout the vast country. Second, the assassination brought about no improvement in Russia's political system. It actually made things worse. Harsh new measures were adopted to stamp out every trace of anti-government activity. Whatever flickering hope for change might have existed under Alexander was now snuffed out altogether.

The men who put so much faith in the gun and the

bomb were believers in anarchism. This political philosophy preaches that all government is evil and must be destroyed. Its originator and prophet, Mikhail Bakunin, expressed both its lofty idealism and its murderous fury: "It is considerably more humane to stab and strangle dozens, nay hundreds, of hated beings," he wrote, than to permit "the torture and martyrdom of millions."

The anarchists believed in "the propaganda of the deed." They hoped that somehow, out of the ruins left by their destructive actions, the people would eventually construct some new, higher, purer form of social organization. Actually most of these revolutionaries were middle- and upper-class intellectuals. They had little contact with the working people and not much genuine understanding of their feelings.

The anarchists' belief that destruction must go on for its own sake until nothing was left of the unjust old system came to be known as nihilism. The term is derived from the Latin word *nihil*, "nothing." For all their passionate commitment and self-sacrifice, that is exactly what the Russian nihilists achieved: *nihil*.

Nevertheless, their failure did not discourage the spread of anarchist violence to other countries. A wave of assassinations swept across Europe. The president of France was slain in 1894, the empress of Austria in 1898, the king of Italy in 1900. The movement reached into the United States as well when an anarchist shot President William McKinley in 1901.

The fateful culmination came in 1914. Archduke Francis Ferdinand of Austria and his wife were shot to death by a young Serbian nationalist. This act triggered the diplomatic turmoil that soon led to the outbreak of World War I.

Meanwhile, in Russia, a new campaign of assassinations had broken out in 1902. This time the killers were members of an organized politcal party, the Socialist Revolutionary party. Over the next decade they assassinated several of the government's highest officials, including the head of the secret police.

The government countered with an extensive use of police spies who infiltrated the revolutionary organizations and exposed their leaders. Hundreds were clapped into prison or exiled to Siberia; others fled abroad.

Despite terror and repression, full-scale revolution broke out in 1905. The czar was compelled to grant a constitution, with provision for a parliament, the Duma. Within weeks the army crushed the rebellion. The new reforms became practically meaningless. On the surface, czarist Russia seemed once again as solid and unyielding as ever.

But change did come. The czarist regime was finally overthrown in 1917. The terrorists could claim little credit for it. The men who carried through the Bolshevik Revolution were of a totally different type. They understood the politics of mass organization and agitation, and they had only scorn for the futile tactics of terrorism.

The Bolsheviks also understood the tactics of ruthless suppression of all opposition. The system these revolutionaries established gradually developed its own elaborate methods for making certain there would be no counterrevolution. The Soviet Union even today contains a vast chain of prison camps and forced-labor camps for the punishment of dissidents.

Yet there is opposition. In recent years there have been some thirty terrorist incidents within the Soviet Union. Soviet aircraft have been hijacked to other countries. There are persistent reports of economic sabotage. But as far as is known, the Soviets have avoided the more violent forms of terrorism. No bombings or assassinations have been reported.

2. The Irish

If Russia was the birthplace of political terrorism, Ireland is the country where nationalist-separatist terrorism first appeared. The Irish struggle against British rule is centuries old.

Organized modern resistance began in 1791, with the formation of the secret Society of United Irishmen. Its supreme effort, the revolt of 1798, was put down without mercy.

For over a century thereafter, the Irish could mount little more than sporadic attacks. A new secret society, the Irish Republican Brotherhood, was formed in 1858. It operated in England as well as in Ireland. One action, the bombing of a London prison in order to free political prisoners, caused so many casualties that the Brotherhood was condemned by the Irish clergy.

Not until 1916 did conditions once more seem favorable for a major insurrection. Britain's armed forces appeared to be fully occupied in World War I.

Irish guerrillas attacked and captured several public buildings in Dublin. Uprisings broke out in numerous

122 THE NEW TERRORISM

other towns. The rebels audaciously declared the independence of the proud new Republic of Ireland. But the battles that eventually became known as the Troubles had only begun.

The British reaction was swifter and more powerful than the Irish had expected. Regular army units were brought in, with artillery. After a week of costly fighting, with many lives lost on both sides and considerable property destruction, the revolt collapsed. Compounding the bitterness of the defeated Irish, the British then executed fourteen of the movement's leaders.

This was almost certainly a tactical error. It only ensured that the surviving nationalists would turn to the last resort of the frustrated extremist, terrorism.

So serious did the new campaign of assassination and arson become in the postwar years that the British had to develop a special new force to deal with it. This paramilitary police force quickly became notorious as the "Black and Tans," a name derived from the colors of the uniforms. The Black and Tans fought the Irish rebels with such unparalleled brutality that even the British public was repelled by it.

The Black and Tan repression failed. It fueled an unquenchable anger—and a veritable holocaust of terrorist reprisals. In a single day known as Bloody Sunday—November 21, 1920—the Irish caught thirteen members of the secret police in their own homes and executed them on the spot.

A political settlement was the only sensible solution. The historic outcome was the British decision to grant independence to a newly created Irish Free State in 1922. This was the first time in all of modern history that so significant a result was won largely by terrorist methods.

But not all of Ireland achieved independence under the new agreement. Protestants form a majority in six of Ireland's northern counties. They had long feared being submerged in a country dominated by Catholics, who vastly outnumber them in the rest of the counties. The mostly Protestant British responded by excluding the five counties from the new republic, keeping them instead within the United Kingdom.

More than sixty years of terrorism has been the result. It has had two root causes: the British rejection of the Irish Catholics' centuries-old aspiration for a united Ireland, and the discriminatory anti-Catholic policies practiced by the Protestant majority in northern Ireland.

The outbreak of World War II in 1939 produced in the IRA the same optimistic reaction that the coming of World War I had evoked among the Irish rebels of that era. Once again the British were fully engaged elsewhere. It seemed the long-hoped-for opportunity to strike the final blow for Irish unity. IRA operations were stepped up, both in Ireland and in England.

The IRA even sent secret agents to obtain aid and support from Hitler's Germany. The Nazis were at first delighted by what seemed a means of striking at Britain through the back door. They promised ample supplies of arms and money. But for reasons that have never been entirely clear, no significant help ever actually reached the IRA.

The next major crisis came in the late 1960s. Inspired by the civil rights movement then at its peak in the United States, the Northern Ireland Civil Rights Association was formed. It attempted to apply the tactics that were proving effective for American blacks. There were demonstrations, protest marches, and acts of nonviolent civil disobedience. The goal was no longer to unite the country but simply to obtain equal rights for the Catholic minority.

The Protestant response was violent. New vigilante groups appeared, the largest being the Ulster Volunteer Force. The Catholic demonstrators and the advocates of civil rights came under savage attack.

Under this intense pressure, the IRA split wide open in January 1970. The Official wing, with its socialist outlook, hoped somehow to bring the country's Catholic and Protestant workers together in the revolutionary struggle against capitalism and imperialism. It therefore opposed the kind of random terrorism that often killed innocent victims and alienated people of both faiths. The leaders of the new Provisional wing were more radical. They called for a heightened campaign of all-out terrorism designed to bring down the government of northern Ireland. Where the Officials relied on traditional fund-raising methods, particularly in America, the Provos robbed so many banks that the government had to set up a costly and elaborate new program of bank security. The Provos also turned to the international network. Soviet-made arms began to flow in from Algeria, Libya, and the Palestinians.

Provo militancy produced a new Protestant backlash. The Protestants formed a new fighting organization, the Ulster Defense Association, which sought to apply the IRA's own terrorist tactics against it. The country was being torn apart as murder and maiming became the order of the day.

The government of northern Ireland collapsed in March 1972. New negotiations began with the British. An acceptable compromise seemed within reach.

Then came Bloody Friday—July 21, 1972. Twenty bombs set by the Provos exploded in Belfast. Nine persons died; 130 were injured. The country was on the verge of chaos.

The British brought in specially picked units of the Regular Army. They have been locked in combat, mostly against the IRA, ever since. The three-sided conflict has mounted to such intensity that by 1976 at least one death was recorded every day.

Yet at that time the total membership of the Official wing was only about a thousand, with about thirteen hundred active members in the Provisional wing. The size of the Protestant forces is not known with any precision. One grisly fact that is known is that the past decade has seen more Catholics killed by Protestant action than the reverse.

Intensive British army campaigns have probably weakened the IRA badly. Many of its top leaders are serving long prison sentences. But the terror goes on. Neither side has enough strength or popular support to win a victory in either the military or the political sense.

Meanwhile emigration from Northern Ireland has proceeded at a pace not seen since the mid-nineteenth-century famine. The region's population has dropped by 10 percent in the past decade. One out of every three university graduates has moved elsewhere. The emigration includes both Catholics and Protestants.

In the words of Thomas O'Hanlon in a recent *Newsday* article, the region has become a "silent, aching hemorrhage."

3. The Jews

Anti-Semitism has been an ugly feature of European life for centuries. The late 1800s witnessed a revival of the ancient hatred in vicious new forms. A German thinker named Karl Eugen Dühring developed a theory asserting that the Jews were different not only in their religion and customs but also in their race. Supposedly they were biologically inferior to the rest of humanity. Therefore, he concluded, they should be totally exterminated.

This theory soon had influential supporters in Germany, France, and England. It was of course adopted and put into murderous practice by the Nazis during World War II.

Starting in 1894, a sensational series of treason trials of a Jewish captain in the French army, Alfred Dreyfus, provoked new storms of anti-Jewish fury. Not until nearly a decade later did the courts declare Dreyfus innocent. He was freed from his solitary prison cell on Devil's Island and restored to his full rank in the army. The irrefutable proof that Dreyfus had been framed probably had little effect on those harboring deep-rooted prejudices.

In Eastern Europe the anti-Semitic revival took the form of mob attacks and mass killing.

Horrified by these events, Jewish leaders began to search for alternatives. A young Viennese journalist, Theodor Herzl, proposed a solution. The Jews must return to their ancient home in the Holy Land. There they would cease to be a constantly persecuted minority; they would become instead a self-governing nation like other nations. This was the dream of Zionism.

Jewish emigration to Palestine, then under British control, was relatively light until World War I. It got a tremendous boost in 1917, when the British government issued the Balfour Declaration. This famous document committed Britain to support "the establishment in Palestine of a national home for the Jewish people."

Over the next twenty years steadily mounting numbers of Jews settled in Palestine. They faced tremendous obstacles. The Palestinian Arabs resented this influx of foreigners. Their resistance became increasingly violent. Yielding to Arab pressure, the British in 1939 placed stringent limits on Jewish immigration.

From the Jewish point of view such restrictions could not have come at a worse time. With the outbreak of World War II, Jews throughout Europe were mortally menaced by the advance of Hitler's armies.

This situation gave rise to Jewish terrorism. A three-sided conflict had developed among the Arabs, the Jews, and the British. Many Jews were convinced that the theoretically neutral British actually favored the Arabs. They pointed to persistent British interference with Jewish self-defense operations.

The Jews' official, though still illegal, fighting force was known as the Haganah ("defense force"). It had long been in action against the Arabs, but refused to attack the British. Small groups of extremists broke away from the Haganah to form their own independent organizations. They were determined to drive the British out of Palestine. Then, they felt sure, the Jews could deal with the Arab threat.

Oldest of the Jewish terrorist forces, formed in the early 1930s, was Irgun Zvai Leumi. The name literally means "national military organization," but it never numbered more than about fifteen hundred fighters. Its founder and commander was Menachem Begin, who later became prime minister of Israel. A smaller and even more fanatical rival group was the so-called Stern Gang.

The Irgun concentrated on property destruction, avoiding killing whenever it could. The Stern Gang, however, carried out a policy of "selective assassination."

Intensified attacks by both groups began in 1944. Military and political installations throughout the country were bombed. British troops suddenly found themselves facing Jewish gunmen.

The climax came in July 1946. An Irgun bomb planted at British headquarters in Jerusalem's King David Hotel killed over a hundred persons, mostly military personnel. Criticized by the Jewish community as well as the rest of the world for this outrage, the Irgun claimed that it always issued warnings to evacuate buildings about to be destroyed. Its message to the King David allegedly got sidetracked.

The bitterness of the struggle is exemplified by another incident. The British some years earlier had decreed the death penalty for anyone caught possessing weapons illegally. The Irgun announced that it would avenge any Jew put to death, whether by the British or by the Palestinians. When the British hanged a nineteen-year-old Irgun fighter, the Irgun executed two young British sergeants it had captured. A majority of Jews protested this brutal act, but the Irgun refused to give up its eye-for-an-eye policy.

By 1947, after the long strain of World War II, Britain was near collapse. It could no longer afford the large and costly armed force required to enforce order in the Holy Land. The British government announced that it would withdraw the troops.

On November 29, 1947, the United Nations took the historic step of voting for a partition of Palestine and the creation of the new state of Israel. In May of the following year, the British forces departed. Arabs and Jews faced one another for the ultimate test of strength.

The war that followed brought an end to Jewish terrorism. The Irgun and the Stern Gang now gave up their separate existences and joined with the Haganah in defense of the new nation. Israel's fighting forces have been united ever since.

Terrorism alone did not create Israel. It was only one of many factors. But it may have been the one that tipped the scale.

4. The Palestinians

Violence against Jewish settlers in Palestine broke out in the early 1920s. The Palestinian Arabs hoped to force a halt to the increased Jewish immigration that resulted from the Balfour Declaration. They particularly resented the Jews' systematic purchase of land and the spread of their agricultural settlements. If this continued, the Palestinians felt, their own people would soon become landless, displaced wanderers.

Major outbreaks of Arab-Jewish fighting occurred in 1929 and again in 1936. British soldiers as well as Jews were attacked. The Palestinians demanded that the British give up their occupation of the Holy Land in favor of a new, independent Palestinian state. A British commission of inquiry then recommended that the country be partitioned between Arabs and Jews.

The Arabs flatly rejected this idea and intensified their attacks. By the onset of World War II in 1939, an estimated fifteen thousand Arab guerrillas were in action. Their tactics were a mixture of guerrilla and terrorist methods, with bombings, arson, and assassinations as well as hit-and-run assaults on isolated Jewish settlements.

During this period the well-known black-and-white checkered headress known as the *kefieh* became the identifying symbol of the Palestinian fighters. These men were called *fedayeen*, an Arabic word that means "self-sacrificers."

The World War II years were marked by almost continual but inconclusive Arab-Jewish fighting. When the two sides were not at each other's throats they turned to strike at the British.

Then, in 1947, came the United Nations vote creating the state of Israel. The ensuing war of 1948 produced some 700,000 Palestinian refugees, scattered around the borders of the new nation. They were to become the seedbed for decades of terrorism. But at first they were disorganized and planless.

In February 1955 Gamal Abdel Nasser, head of the new nationalist Egyptian government, announced that he would assist the Palestinian fedayeen with training and arms. Raids against the Israelis were soon on the increase.

One of those who benefited from Egyptian aid was a young Palestinian named Yasir Arafat. The Egyptian army trained him as a demolition expert, giving expertise with explosives that would be especially useful for a future terrorist chieftain. During the brief Egyptian-Israeli war of 1956, Arafat fought as a lieutenant in the Egyptian army.

The following year he organized Al Fatah ("Conquest" or "Victory"), a fedayee force committed to the reconquest of Palestine. The group was not strong enough to launch its first operation until late in 1964. One reason for the delay was that the Palestinians were badly divided among themselves. Factionalism was an Arab problem of long standing.

An Arab summit meeting in Cairo in 1964 proved fateful for the Palestinians. The Arab governments voted for the creation of a new group, the Palestine Liberation Organization. Each government would contribute to its support. The new PLO was meant to serve as an umbrella body in which the frequently feuding Palestinian factions could work out their differences and unite for the common cause. The PLO's sworn goal, explicitly stated in its constitution, was all-out war for the destruction of Israel.

In its early years the PLO was dominated and controlled by the Egyptians. Arafat and his Al Fatah had meanwhile obtained the support of the Syrian government.

Through the late 1960s Al Fatah was the most active of the Palestinian factions. Its raids and bombings kept the Israelis off balance. It was soon the largest and strongest fedayee group. Recognition came in 1969 when Arafat was elected chairman of the PLO while retaining his post as head of Al Fatah.

But the Palestinian tradition of factionalism was still strong. Some politically radical Palestinians regarded Arafat as a political conservative and compromiser. To these believers in Marxist-Leninist theory, he was too exclusively concerned with regaining the lost homeland. Arafat rejected their insistence on the need to organize and indoctrinate the Palestinian poor for the eventual socialist revolution.

The first break came in 1968 when two young physicians, George Habash and Waddih Haddad, formed the radical Popular Front for the Liberation of Palestine. Even this group's dedication to communist dogma was insufficient for some of the extremists, however. In 1969, led by the ultra-radical Naif Hawatmeh, they broke away to form the Popular Democratic Front for the Liberation of Palestine. At about the same time a more conservative group of former army officers, led by Ahmed Jibril, set up its own Popular Front for the Liberation of Palestine–General Command. Each of these groups subsequently conducted its own terrorist campaigns against Israel.

By 1970 the Palestinian resistance had reached a peak of strength. It had enlisted a total of about twenty thousand fighters, though only about half of these were trained and fully armed as yet. But 1970 was to prove a year of disaster.

A large part of the PLO force was based in Jordan at that time. King Hussein distrusted the increasingly arrogant and demanding Palestinians. Then came the PLO's biggest operation, the skyjacking of four airliners in a single day. Three of the planes were flown to an airport outside the Jordanian capital of Amman, and they were ultimately blown up there.

Neither the king nor anyone in his government had been consulted about this operation, nor had they been asked for permission to use Jordanian territory. Hussein ordered his army to drive out the Palestinians. The resulting battles were fierce, but the Palestinians could not stand up against the well-equipped and disciplined Jordanian army. Thousands of them were killed, and the rest were forced to flee the country. Most moved to Lebanon, which then became the main base for PLO recruitment, training, and operations.

The early 1970s saw persistent Palestinian raids against targets in Israel, countered by a steady toughening of Israeli security measures. By the middle of the decade any such operation was acknowledged to be a suicide action. The fedayeen who volunteered for such a raid were revered as dead heroes from the moment they went on the mission. By the late 1970s the Palestinians were operating almost exclusively against targets outside Israel, such as airline offices, aircraft, and diplomatic facilities. From their sanctuary in Lebanon they periodically shelled towns and villages in northern Israel.

Meanwhile, Arafat was demonstrating extraordinary skill in diplomacy and the manipulation of world opinion. As we have seen, he persuaded nations around the world to bestow official recognition on the PLO as the sole representative of the Palestinian people. His 1974 address to the United Nations General Assembly marked the emergence of the PLO as a factor in world politics. Thereafter, in vote after vote in the General Assembly on issues relating to Palestine, large majorities invariably sided with the PLO. By the early 1980s the Palestinian cause seemed to be moving, painfully at times but inexorably, toward fulfillment.

All this was changed by the shattering Israeli invasion of Lebanon in 1982. The PLO's quick defeat—despite the funds, military supplies, and years of training lavished on the organization—gravely disappointed its allies. Nearly ten thousand PLO fighters were dispersed to Arab countries throughout the Middle East and North Africa. Suddenly the entire destiny of the up-rooted Palestinian people was once again in question.

Years would be required for rebuilding and restoring the PLO to anything resembling its former prestige and military power. Some observers wondered whether such a restoration would ever be possible. Renewed terrorism seemed likely; but its effectiveness was problematical.

And yet, the Palestinian problem remained alive. The thousands in the wretched refugee camps had not disappeared. They were a thorn in the conscience of the world.

5. The Uruguayans

Terrorism in Latin America is of more recent date than that in any other part of the world. It developed there in the late 1950s. Nowhere was its rise and fall more dramatic than in Uruguay.

This small country of about three million people was exceptional in several ways. In a continent dominated by repressive military dictatorships, with extremely wide divisions between rich and poor, Uruguay was an island of democracy and prosperity. It boasted a large and well-educated middle class and a generally literate population.

Starting in 1958 the Uruguayan economy began to falter. A burgeoning inflation drained away purchasing power. Industrial production began to slow down, and spreading unemployment caused distress among the people. A series of government scandals revealed widespread corruption.

Young middle-class professionals and intellectuals were hit especially hard. There seemed to be no future for them. They began to search for radical solutions.

Some of them were profoundly moved by the wretched living and working conditions of the most impoverished group in the country, the migrant farm workers. They hit on the idea of hijacking trucks carrying food to the cities and then distributing the food among these needy folk. This was the humble birth of the terrorist movement that almost wrecked Uruguayan society.

The farm workers' response was understandably enthusiastic. From that moment on, they could always be counted on to give whatever aid they could to the radicals. As the news spread, networks of sympathizers began to develop in the cities as well.

The militants did not give their new movement its formal name until 1965: Movimiento de Liberacion Nacional (National Liberation Movement). They were already better known as the Tupamaros, after an Inca

chieftain and national hero, Tupac Amaru, who had
fought the Spanish conquistadores in the eighteenth
century.

The new movement was both nationalistic and
socialistic. Its leader, Raul Sendic, and his followers were
convinced that the nation's problems stemmed mainly
from excessive foreign economic influence. The most
powerful of these "imperialist" influences was the
United States. Two tasks were therefore to be accomplished: the American imperialists must be driven out,
and the groundwork must be laid for the inevitable,
violent socialist revolution.

The Tupamaros' history as an armed fighting force
began in July 1963 when they attacked a sports club and
seized a dozen automatic rifles. There were no more
than twenty people in the movement at that time. Two
years later it had about five hundred full-time activists
and perhaps ten times that many sympathizers. At the
peak of its power in 1971 the Tupamaro force could
muster three thousand totally committed fighters.

The Tupamaros placed more emphasis than most
terrorist organizations on winning the people over to
their side. They would sometimes seize control of a theater full of people or a factory crowded with workers for
the sole purpose of explaining their cause to these cap-
tive audiences. They would temporarily occupy broadcast facilities so that the revolutionary message could
have broader impact. The revolutionaries also developed their own extensive press.

Fund-raising was carried out in traditional terrorist
style, by robberies and kidnappings. Banks were an obvious target, but the Tupamaros made a special point of

hitting the fashionable gambling casinos too. This seemed a delightful way of forcing the rich to support the struggle in behalf of the poor.

Kidnappings of major Uruguayan political and business leaders became almost commonplace, yielding sizable ransoms. But in accordance with their anti-imperialist aims, the Tupamaros also abducted a number of foreign diplomats and executives working with some of the big multinational corporations with headquarters in Montevideo.

Police efforts to suppress the movement only aroused its fury. Tupamaro killers assassinated so many police officers that for a time some members of the police actually refused to appear for work in their uniforms.

By the middle of 1971 the Tupamaros seemed on the verge of taking power. Public opinion polls taken around this time showed that six Uruguayans out of ten sympathized with them.

An election was scheduled early the following year. In September 1971 the Tupamaros decided to suspend all violent actions so that the election campaign could proceed peacefully over the next five months. They were certain their candidate would win easily.

They were wrong. The candidate favored by the ruling establishment won.

The Tupamaros tried to renew their attacks more vigorously than ever, but during the five-month lull the army and the police had been preparing a comprehensive anti-terrorist plan. They swung into action as soon as the election was over. Swift nationwide raids and a number of pitched battles resulted in disaster for the Tupamaros. Many were killed, and some five thousand were arrested. The Tupamaro movement had been broken.

The victory over terrorism had its dark side. The government's grant of virtually unlimited powers to the military authorities was meant to be temporary, but Uruguay today is still a military dictatorship. No one can predict when, or whether, South America's unique former democracy will ever regain its once proud status.

6.   The Americans

Some historians trace a terrorist tradition in the United States back to the era of the American Revolution. They point to the Boston Tea Party as an operation that fits the definition: a carefully planned, highly dramatic act of violence, staged not so much for its own sake as for its effect on the government. Also terroristic in nature was the vicious fighting that took place in many colonies between rebel patriots and loyalists. There were assassinations, kidnappings, tar-and-featherings, and widespread arson.

Later the lawless conditions of life on the western frontier gave rise to a peculiarly American form of terrorism. Fear and violence were used in behalf of law and order. Settlers beset by gunslingers, cattle rustlers, and outlaws of every stripe organized their own temporary law-enforcement groups—the vigilantes. They took it upon themselves to hunt down lawbreakers and punish them, sometimes by whipping but most often by hanging. At least five hundred persons are known to have been executed by vigilantes between 1860 and 1910.

The post–Civil War period also produced terrorist violence, mostly against blacks. Southern whites, determined to keep the emancipated slaves in a position of inferiority, organized for repression. The Ku Klux Klan was formed in Tennessee in 1867. Similar groups appeared elsewhere and were soon spreading terror throughout the South. A congressional investigation reported that over 150 blacks had been killed in a single county in Florida in 1871. Twice that number had been murdered in the area around New Orleans.

This racist violence was not aimed solely at blacks, however. Whites sympathetic to the black struggle for equality were flogged and driven out of the South, or killed.

With the South fully restored to white dominance by the mid-1870s, the Klan faded into relative inactivity. It was revived in 1915 in reaction to the rise of a new militancy among blacks.

Within a decade the Klan could boast an estimated five million members throughout the country. Its new power was graphically demonstrated in 1925 when Klan members were allowed to parade in their hoods and robes on Pennsylvania Avenue, in Washington, D.C., the thoroughfare that passes right by the White House.

Klan violence in the 1920s and 1930s was directed not only against blacks but against Catholics and Jews as well. Labor organizers were another favorite target. But blacks remained the prime victims. An estimated fifteen hundred black persons were lynched annually during these years.

The civil rights movement of the 1950s and 1960s

caused a new upsurge of racist terror. Cross burnings, bombings, and murders made headlines across the country. Both blacks and whites were prey to the new brutality.

The Klan in recent years has turned increasingly to action against anti-war and anti-nuclear protesters and other political dissenters. Rising Klan membership, influence, and finances boded ill for the 1980s.

Terrorism of a different type marked the early years of the American labor movement. Both management and labor resorted to violence to achieve their ends.

The Pennsylvania coal fields became the scene of a near–civil war in the late 1860s and 1870s. The miners saw that their attempts to organize for better wages and working conditions met only harsh treatment at the hands of the mine owners and their notorious "coal-and-iron police." The miners formed a new secret society named the Molly Maguires, after a heroine of the Irish peasants' struggle against the landlords. The Mollies beat and killed a number of mine bosses and sabotaged several mines.

An undercover detective named Jamie McParlan infiltrated the organization. His testimony helped convict its leaders and most active members. Ten were executed. Others received long prison sentences.

If the Mollies had brought their ideas with them from Ireland, other American labor forces were influenced by other doctrines imported from Europe. The theories of Bakunin and his anarchist followers and those of Karl Marx and the socialists both shaped the ongoing struggle.

One of America's earliest and most influential advocates of terrorist action in the anarchist tradition was a German immigrant who arrived in 1883. Johann Most, editor of the German-language radical newspaper *Freiheit* and duly elected member of the German Reichstag, had been forced into exile because of his open advocacy of revolutionary violence. He reestablished his paper in New York City and continued his inflammatory propaganda.

Most's newspaper unashamedly defended robbery by revolutionaries on the ground that "year in and year out the working people are robbed of everything but the bare necessities of life." The revolutionary therefore has every right to "confiscate at least as much as he is able to of what has been created by workers."

At one time Most obtained work in a Jersey City explosives factory under a false name. He used the knowledge he gained from this job to write a pamphlet, *The Science of Revolutionary War,* which was nothing less than a detailed handbook on the making of bombs. It gives step-by-step, do-it-yourself directions for making nitroglycerine as well as for committing arson and burglary and for using poisons.

Other anarchist publications of the 1880s were equally candid in their enthusiasm for explosives. A letter that appeared in one extremist paper, *Alarm,* exclaimed:

> Dynamite! Of all the good stuff, this is the stuff. . . . Place this in the immediate vicinity of a lot of rich loafers who live by the sweat of other people's brows, and light the fuse. A most cheerful and gratifying result will follow.

Radical propaganda of this kind had a growing popular appeal in the last decades of the nineteenth century. Chicago at this time supported no less than five anarchist newspapers. Their readership totaled a quarter of a million.

The authorities were understandably alarmed. Some way had to be found to counter the spread of extremism.

In May 1886, during a long and bitter strike at the McCormick Harvester plant, Chicago police fired into the crowd of pickets, killing or wounding half a dozen. Thousands attended a protest meeting in Haymarket Square the next night. When the police advanced on the meeting to break it up, someone threw a bomb into their midst and killed seven police officers. Other officers retaliated by firing into the crowd, killing many of the demonstrators. This event became celebrated as the Haymarket Massacre.

Eight anarchists were arrested, tried for murder, and convicted. No proof was introduced to show that they had committed the bombing. The judge accepted the argument that the anarchists' constant incitement to revolutionary violence made them as guilty as if they had. Four of the accused were eventually executed. For years afterward, the entire American labor movement was unfairly saddled with charges of instigating such incidents.

The two streams of socialism and anarchism converged briefly in 1905 with the formation of the Industrial Workers of the World. The IWW, whose members were popularly known as Wobblies, sought to unionize the unskilled, chiefly immigrant workers who were being neglected by the American Federation of Labor. Its founders were "Big Bill" Heywood, president of the Western Federation of Miners; Daniel De Leon, head of the Socialist Labor party; and Eugene V. Debs, leader of the Socialist party. The IWW soon split, as the socialists favored peaceable political action while Heywood and his followers advocated "direct action" in the anarchist style. Once the socialists had departed, the IWW concentrated on strikes and sabotage.

IWW policies did not extend to violence against human life, but that did not prevent the anarchists from being blamed for three bombings that took a large number of innocent lives. On October 1, 1910, the *Los Angeles Times* building was destroyed by dynamite. Twenty persons died; seventeen were injured. Two young ironworkers eventually confessed to this crime.

Another bomb explosion during a Preparedness Day parade in San Francisco took nine lives on July 22, 1916. Two IWW leaders were convicted in this case and served long prison terms, but evidence uncovered later indicated that they had probably been framed.

On September 16, 1920, a tremendous explosion in New York's Wall Street killed forty and injured three hundred. Ironically almost all of those who died were ordinary working people; not a single wealthy or powerful person was hurt. Intensive investigation failed to discover the perpetrators, and no one was ever formally charged. Credit for it had been claimed by an otherwise unknown group calling itself the American Anarchist Fighters.

Far from promoting the cause of revolution, this wave of bombings was a factor in provoking a coast-to-coast anti-radical campaign by federal, state, and local governments. Over four thousand persons were arrested as suspected extremists during this so-called Red Scare of 1919–21. Several hundred who were not U.S. citizens were deported, but most of the others had to be released for lack of evidence.

Anarchist-style terrorism then took a forty-year holiday in America. It reappeared in the 1960s.

As the Vietnam War lengthened without seeming any closer to a victorious end, disillusionment and anger spread across the nation's college campuses. The principal organization expressing the young people's unrest was the rapidly growing Students for a Democratic Society (SDS). With only two thousand members in 1965, SDS had thirty thousand by 1968 in chapters at three hundred colleges and universities. But its leadership was badly divided between moderates and extremists.

At the national convention of SDS in June 1969, the radicals won control of the organization. The two top leaders, Mark Rudd and Bernadine Dohrn, appropriated the SDS mailing list, funds, and national office in Chicago. These were used to lay the basis for a new underground force, the Weatherman organization (the "man" in "Weatherman" was dropped later because of protests by feminist members; the group became the Weather Underground).

The new group published a 25,000-word communiqué pledging to fight for world revolution against "Amerikan [sic] imperialism." It suffered disaster almost at once when one of its bomb factories in a Greenwich Village townhouse blew up in March 1970, killing three members. Two others, Kathy Boudin and Cathlyn Wilkerson, managed to escape from the ruins despite the fact that they had suffered serious injuries and had their clothes virtually blown off.

Throughout the early 1970s, the Weather People conducted a sustained campaign of terror. Their first major operation was a bombing of New York City police headquarters in May 1970, only two months after the Greenwich Village accident. By 1975 the group had claimed twenty-seven bombings. Its targets included the U.S. Capitol, the Pentagon, the State Department, banks, corrections offices, police stations, and the offices of several multinational corporations. Total property damage was estimated at about $10 million.

In all their operations, the Weather People were careful to avoid hurting anyone. Their bombs exploded at times when the targeted buildings were unoccupied.

Weather Underground membership by early 1976 was estimated at between fifty and two hundred. It was then the largest of all terrorist groups in the United States. A West Coast counterpart, the New World Liberation Front, could boast only about twenty-five members in three active units at that time.

But the mid-1970s represented the peak of the Weather group's strength. Within five years many of its leaders either surrendered to or were apprehended by the authorities. The number of Weather Underground attacks declined sharply. The failure of the 1981 Brink's robbery may have marked its final attempt to resume the battle.

Ultra-leftist conspiracies still persisted in the United States. Tiny new groups kept surfacing. In one mid-1982 raid in San Jose, California, police discovered blueprints for the armory alarm systems of the U.S. Army depot at the Presidio in San Francisco. A band calling itself the Well Springs Commune had apparently plotted to steal arms and explosives. Four members were arrested. One who got away was Marilyn Jean Buck, last of the Brink's robbery fugitives still at large.

IX.

FLASHFORWARD: TOMORROW'S CHILLING POSSIBILITIES

Three horrifying possibilities loom ahead. Terrorists may lay their hands on nuclear, chemical, or biological weapons within the next few years. An act of mass destruction costing hundreds of thousands or even millions of lives would then become a real danger.

There is a fourth possibility. It might be less murderous, but could be disastrous for the maintenance of social order. It would take the form of large-scale technological disruption.

1. The Nuclear Threat

Terrorists could gain possession of nuclear materials in any of several ways. The most obvious method is by stealing either a nuclear weapon or the material needed to make one. This could be done at a manufacturing plant, a nuclear power plant, a military base, a weapons storage area, or while the materials are in transit from one place to another.

147

Nuclear installations around the world today are surprisingly vulnerable to terrorist action. A U.S. Senate report warned in 1972 that security in the North Atlantic Treaty Organization nuclear weapons bases scattered throughout Western Europe was totally inadequate. Ten years later half of these installations had not yet been reinforced. According to *The New York Times*, May 9, 1982, both the CIA and the Joint Chiefs of Staff stated that these sites were poorly protected and could easily be attacked by terrorists or demonstrators.

A seminar held at the Pentagon in December 1981 pointed to one nuclear facility where a few well-organized raiders could penetrate the weapons bunker within two minutes. Other installations were poorly lit at night, their fencing was often rusty or broken, and their alarm systems were unreliable. Exercises held by the U.S. Army's Green Berets in 1975 had revealed that even those facilities adequately equipped with guards, fences, and sensors could be invaded. The attackers were unlikely to be detected until it was too late.

A comprehensive program for eliminating these weaknesses had been launched in 1973. It was supposed to be completed by 1980. Revised recent estimates projected completion some time in the mid-1980s.

Nuclear security experts are realistic enough to admit that total security is unattainable. Even the finest and most complete safeguard systems have weak points. A dozen determined, properly trained, powerfully equipped raiders could almost certainly penetrate any conceivable set of defenses. The most that can be done is to confront the terrorists with systems that delay them until overwhelming force can be brought to bear against them.

Stealing nuclear materials from which a bomb could be fabricated would probably be easier than acquiring a completed weapon. The specific material needed is plutonium oxide, or plutonium 239. Operating nuclear plants constantly extract this material from their enriched-uranium fuel. The plutonium is then molded into spherical pellets no more than half an inch in diameter. These are usually packed into containers about the size of ordinary coffee cans. They must then be transported to isolated storage areas, often at some distance.

Hijacking one of the trucks that carry these materials would pose few serious problems for a well-planned raid. Some carry neither guards nor secure, robbery-proof container compartments. The transportation phase is the most vulnerable aspect of the nuclear industry.

Plutonium could also be pilfered by someone employed in a nuclear facility. The insider would need to take only a tiny, easily concealable quantity each day. A gradual accumulation of about twenty pounds of plutonium would suffice for a bomb powerful enough to destroy the center of an average city.

There is little question that terrorists would be able to produce a homemade but effective nuclear weapon once they had the materials. The world was made uncomfortably aware of how easy this could be through a television documentary aired on the Public Broadcasting System in 1975.

The producers of the documentary gave a young university student the task of creating a feasible bomb design. It took him exactly five weeks. He proved that all the required information was easily available in published form. Besides the plutonium and a substantial amount of conventional explosives, the only materials needed could be purchased at any hardware store or from other legal, commercial sources.

Under certain circumstances it might not be necessary to make a bomb. Plutonium is one of the most toxic substances known. The mere threat to release a quantity of it in a densely populated area would compel the authorities to treat terrorists' demands with utmost seriousness.

Making such a threat believable would be relatively simple. The plutonium could be converted into a mist or spray. A few ounces dispersed into the intake of a large building's air-conditioning system would suffice to contaminate the entire building and kill or incapacitate every person inside.

Still another alternative is the seizure of a nuclear plant. The attackers could then threaten to release radioactive emissions into the atmosphere. Such a warning might actually be more credible than the menace of a nuclear weapon. Technically trained members of a raiding team could maintain close control over the emissions, releasing as much or as little as seemed likely to force compliance with their demands.

Although it is clear that terrorists do have the capability to threaten nuclear devastation in one form or another, it is less certain that they would carry out such a threat. In the words of Robert A. Fearey, former U.S. State Department coordinator for combatting terrorism,

> Terrorists, at least the rational ones, fundamentally seek to influence people, not to kill them. The death of

thousands or tens of thousands of persons could produce a tremendous backlash.

This does not mean that the possibility can be ruled out. The percentage of terrorist incidents in which more than one person was killed multiplied more than ten times between 1970 and 1980. This statistic is still another reflection of the tendency among today's terrorists to kill senselessly and indiscriminately. A gang sufficiently desperate or commanded by a deranged leader could be capable of limitless horror.

"Rational" terrorists, as Fearey correctly states, would probably not commit such an act. But not all terrorists are rational.

The danger is rendered more alarming by the persistent efforts of Libyan dictator Muammar Qaddafi to obtain the materials and technology needed to produce nuclear weapons. At least one European arms dealer was reported in 1982 to have offered Libya a nuclear reactor, weapons designs, and a nuclear reprocessing plant for the production of plutonium.

Qaddafi has been closely linked to the radical groups in the Palestinian movement, particularly the PFLP. If this unstable person were to obtain nuclear materials, the risk of a nuclear holocaust would escalate enormously.

2. The Chemical Threat

Poison gas. Teargas. Nerve gas. Nauseating gas. Blistering and burning gas. "Yellow rain." Crop-killing and jungle-killing sprays.

Some take effect when inhaled. With others, a few

drops on the skin are all that is needed. Still others attack the eyes. All have demonstrated their capacity for killing or incapacitating. All are potentially vulnerable to terrorist theft or manufacture.

From the terrorist point of view, chemical weapons have certain advantages over nuclear weapons. They are less carefully guarded. They are easier to obtain or manufacture, to conceal, and to transport. Relatively small quantities can have potent effects.

Properly packaged chemicals are also far less hazardous to those handling them than are radioactive nuclear materials. Danger does threaten at the moment when they are dispersed into the atmosphere, however. Terrorists would require protective gear.

According to Robert Kupperman and Darrell Trent in their 1979 study, *Terrorism: Threat, Reality, Response*, two types of chemical agents would probably be easiest for terrorists either to acquire or to make for themselves. These are known technically as the fluoroacetates and the organophosphorous compounds.

The fluoroacetates are commonly found in rat poisons. They kill by preventing the cells of a living organism from carrying out their normal functions. The organophosphorous agents attack the nervous system. They are found in many widely used insecticides.

Terrorist use of such weapons would require a practical method for disseminating them rapidly over a large, populated area. The authorities would have to be convinced that the attackers were really capable of carrying out the threat. The technical difficulties and dangers involved may be the reasons why no such threat has yet been attempted.

Another, seemingly simpler method that is often mentioned is the use of some chemical poison to contaminate an urban water-supply system. This would actually be more difficult than it sounds. In order to have an effect that was not extremely local or short-lived, huge quantities of the poison would have to be fed into the system at a number of knowledgeably selected points. Detection would otherwise be too rapid for the effect to spread very far. The affected parts of the system could be shut down with relative ease until the poisons could be flushed out.

3. The Biological Threat

Accusations of germ warfare have been leveled on several recent occasions. Newly released World War II documents indicate that the Japanese experimented on Chinese prisoners of war with certain infectious diseases. In the early 1950s the North Koreans charged, with very little evidence, that the United States had attempted to spread epidemics during the Korean War. The Russians were reported in 1981 to have employed biological agents in Afghanistan.

The number of diseases that can at least theoretically be spread by artificial means is large. Two in particular seem possible, though still unlikely, candidates for terrorist use.

One is botulism. This almost always fatal form of food poisoning is normally caused by improperly canned or smoked food. The symptoms are produced by a nerve toxin, which in turn is the product of bacteria developing within deteriorating foods. Kupperman and Trent state that the botulinal toxin is "a thousand times more effective" than the most toxic nerve agents that could be manufactured by purely chemical processes.

Far more practical and effective than botulism is pulmonary anthrax. The spore that carries this disease is "the most available, yet devastating agent within the reach of terrorists." Anthrax symptoms are similar to those of pneumonia. If untreated, it is nearly 100 percent fatal. Massive penicillin doses are the only known treatment. A grave complication stems from the fact that the symptoms do not appear immediately, so that the infected population might not be aware it had been attacked. By the time the symptoms did appear, antibiotic therapy would be useless.

The anthrax spore is exceptionally hardy. It has been known to survive for decades under extremely unfavorable conditions. It could be cultivated quite easily by anyone with reasonable biochemical training and simple equipment.

A skillfully conducted anthrax attack on an urban population of about five million would probably kill about 600,000 people. A death rate of this magnitude would be comparable to that likely to be caused by certain types of nuclear attacks.

The problem here, as with the chemical agents, is finding a method for directing these biological agents into a target area in such a way as to ensure the maximum effect. Systematic measures would have to be taken to protect those using them.

One possibility is an aerosol spray from a helicopter or low-flying airplane operating somewhat in the manner of the crop-dusting planes that sprinkle insecticides on farm areas. Another is some type of bomb or artillery shell that would spread the infection when it exploded in the target area. These technically demanding methods seem beyond the means of most terrorist groups. Certainly the possibilities have been well known for a long time; the fact remains that the extremists have thus far not tried them.

4. The Technological Threat

Modern society is an intertwined and interdependent system. Its smooth day-to-day operation relies on fragile, complex technologies. These are subject to interference by an almost infinite variety of methods.

The most familiar example is the airlines. Attacks have been almost too numerous to count during the past three decades. Relatively few have involved bombs planted aboard airliners, but such devices have produced catastrophic explosions on several flights.

Hijackings have been far more numerous. Stern countermeasures by the countries whose airlines have been most often affected have reduced the frequency of such actions but have by no means eliminated them. Their frequency was still mounting as the 1970s ended. According to Anthony Quainton, August 1980 "enters into the Guinness book of terrorist records as the month with the most hijackings, all of American aircraft."

Operations against airlines have effects that reach far beyond the immediate victims. Airports around the world have had to institute complex and extremely costly security procedures. Millions of passengers have had to accustom themselves to metal detectors, X-ray examinations of baggage, and other bothersome steps. They have also had to bear the added costs.

Some experts point to the world's oil and gas pipelines as a second category of vulnerable technology. Extending for many thousands of miles in many parts of the world, often passing through barren and uninhabited terrain, they would seem to offer abundant opportunities for assault. And in reality these lines have been cut many times. Results have not been encouraging for the attackers.

The pipelines are not actually a target well suited to the purposes of terrorism. Interruptions of pipeline flow are certainly a nuisance, but they can be repaired or bypassed fairly quickly and easily.

The mere threat to blow up a section of pipeline has rarely if ever yielded any considerable concessions either by the companies directly affected or by their governments. Such an explosion could hardly be expected to affect world oil supplies to any major extent. For that, major campaigns of sustained and extensive destruction would be required. No terrorist group has yet shown itself capable of so protracted an effort.

A different part of the oil industry is sometimes mentioned as another potential target: the offshore oil rigs. Their relative isolation could expose them to bomb threats, with the workers held hostage. The situation would be roughly comparable to that aboard a hijacked airliner. Attempts to rescue the hostages and apprehend the attackers would be inhibited by the difficulty of approaching the target without triggering the terrorists' threatened response.

The raiders' problem would also be difficult. The

bomb would probably have to be planted on the rig by someone employed there, since strangers have no access to it. Or the terrorists would have to mount some sort of assault by plane, helicopter, or fast boat. They would have to win control of the rig and the people on it. They could then place their explosives and announce their demands.

Such an attack from outside is conceivable, but seems improbable. It would certainly require facilities not readily available to most terrorist organizations. Considering the hazards and complexities involved, it is not surprising that no serious attempt has yet been made against an oil rig. Security officers have nevertheless prepared elaborate precautions against this potentially costly eventuality.

A much more logical and accessible target exists in the electric power generating and transmission systems on which the world depends for so much of its energy needs. These have been attacked in many countries and on many occasions.

Electric power systems are open to attack at a number of key points: the big power plants, the high-voltage transformer substations, and the major switching centers. These are so numerous that they can be only lightly protected. Moreover, their machinery and equipment are quite delicate and easily damaged. Repair or replacement is a time-consuming process and a very expensive one.

The most visible targets, the many thousands of miles of high-tension towers and power lines, are also the most vulnerable. Attacks at well-chosen points have caused major difficulties. In August 1982 guerrillas blacked out the entire eastern half of El Salvador for several days. At about the same time dynamiters in Peru cut off electricity to Lima and several other cities.

A well-coordinated assault on a few carefully selected power plants and substations could have drastic and lasting effects. Entire metropolitan areas, even entire regions, would suffer prolonged power outages. The lives of thousands, perhaps millions of ordinary citizens would be seriously disrupted. Industrial production throughout the affected area would come to a sudden halt. So would essential services such as broadcast communications and electric-powered transportation, lighting, heating and cooling systems, elevators in high-rise buildings, and food-storage facilities. Society would face the probability of serious social disorder.

A long-lasting blackout could give terrorists an opportunity to profit from the situation in other ways. With the forces of law and order engaged against criminals, the terrorists could strike at government centers, major industrial plants, financial institutions, communication and transportation centers, and other targets.

Telephone systems would seem another natural target, but only one major attack has been reported so far. In April 1982 suspected Basque terrorists posing as police planted six bombs in a Madrid telephone exchange. An estimated 700,000 lines were knocked out. Communications inside Spain and with other countries were crippled for several days.

Newer than these as an essential element in today's society are the world's interlocked computer systems. They are increasingly crucial to its efficient functioning. Political affairs, military matters, economic activity, scientific and technological processes, and other basic aspects of modern living could be impaired by a major penetration and disruption of the computer networks.

The susceptibility of these systems to manipulation by trained specialists has been demonstrated in a number of well-publicized criminal cases. These have usually involved attempts to defraud banks or large corporations of substantial amounts of money.

Terrorists might well attempt a similar operation. A successful financial swindle on a big scale would constitute a real fund-raising coup.

But other objectives might offer even greater profit. Political intelligence records stored in computer memories would be one prime target. Records relating to the terrorists themselves or to planning for antiterrorist operations could be altered or erased. Covert espionage operations could be discovered and revealed to the countries being spied on.

Military intelligence data banks could be another vital objective. An enemy country's top-secret plans and records could be copied and passed on to a friendly government. Significant changes could be introduced into the stored data to confuse and distort planning for military operations.

Computer intrusions by well-versed experts could be especially disruptive for a nation's financial and economic life. With millions of transactions recorded every day, the possibilities for paralyzing essential functions both within a targeted country and on the international scene are nearly endless.

Major penetrations of computer systems presuppose high levels of technical mastery. So far as is known, no terrorist organization has yet acquired the requisite skills. The risk remains, however, and cannot be ignored. Bribery of key personnel is one of several possibilities.

Modern science and technology have become such an accustomed part of our lives that we tend to take their miracles for granted. They stand as towering triumphs of human creativity. Only time will tell whether fanatical groups will yet turn them against society in ways that are as yet only partly imaginable.

X.

HOW TO COMBAT TERRORISM

The dilemma will be to break the few dozens of [terrorists] without eroding the liberties of the millions of innocent people, and to prevent or punish violence without stifling legitimate protest—Richard L. Clutterbuck, *Protest and the Urban Guerrilla* (1973).

Terrorism can be stopped. Considerable progress has already been accomplished.

In Italy nearly two thousand militants were imprisoned in the early 1980s. In West Germany relentless police offensives virtually destroyed the once-powerful Baader-Meinhof Gang and the Red Army Faction. The Japanese Red Army was driven from its native soil and now exists only as a shrunken dependent of the PFLP. In the United States only isolated remnants of the Weather Underground, the Symbionese Liberation Army, and the Black Liberation Army are still at large. In the Middle East the PLO suffered shattering reverses.

In South America, too, a kind of victory was won, but at a heavy price. The revolutionaries succeeded in bringing on the ruthless repression that they believed would provoke the people to rise up in revolt. Instead, it

161

fastened the yoke of semi-fascist dictatorship on virtually the entire continent. Terrorism is almost dead
there, but so is liberty.

Much still remains to be done. Activist groups continue their deadly operations in many parts of the
world. New ones seem to spring forth almost as fast as
the older ones are crushed. The IRA, the Basques, the
Corsicans, the feuding Muslim sects, the Armenians, the
anti-Castro Cubans, the European neo-fascists and
neo-Nazis, the ultra-left in France, the as yet only par-
tially damaged Milan, Rome, and Naples columns of the
Red Brigades, the Ku Klux Klan, the American Nazis,
the Jewish Defense League—these are only some of the
gangs that are still making headlines.

The question is not whether terrorism can be reduced, but how to reduce it further and eventually
eliminate it. What specific steps can and should be tak-
en? Equally important, what steps should be avoided?

1.   Prevention and Deterrence

The most fundamental preventive measure is the elimi-
nation of injustice. The causes that terrorists seize upon
and exploit for their own purposes are often rooted in
genuine grievances. Wherever large numbers of people
are kept in poverty and ignorance, wherever minorities
groan under oppression, wherever national homelands
are under foreign rule, wherever human rights are
trampled, wherever governments cannot or will not deal
with deepening economic crisis, the seeds of revolutionary terrorism are being sown.

In some countries, even peaceable and gradual efforts

to alleviate these problems have stirred up an ultra-rightist backlash. Violence in defense of existing evils cannot be allowed to stifle progress.

Right-wing extremists often rely on racial, religious, and ethnic prejudices to inflame their followers. Two antidotes can be applied. One consists of long-term, comprehensive educational campaigns aimed at improving relations among all elements of society. The other takes the form of determined action against those who incite or commit violence against minorities.

Measures directed at the causes of terrorism must be backed up by steps aimed against its means of action. A first, obvious step would seem to be cutting off all access to weapons. Despite serious efforts by many governments and international organizations, this has turned out to be almost impossible.

It has been suggested, for example, that the purchase of explosives be restricted. Companies manufacturing and selling explosives would be required to keep strict records of all sales, with severe punishment for illegal or improper distribution of these materials. The trouble is that regulations of this type have rarely been effective. They are relatively easy to evade. No practical method to enforce such restrictions has yet been devised. Nor is there any way to prevent people from purchasing the materials for making explosives.

Efforts to regulate the flow of small arms, from pistols and revolvers to rifles and automatic weapons, face similar difficulties. Methods exist for the detection of illicit shipments, such as X-ray and metal-detecting equipment. Extra-rigorous customs inspections have also had some effect. But with the international arms traffic burgeoning as never before, with billions of dollars' worth of weapons constantly crossing borders, substantial quantities will inevitably find their way through illegal channels into terrorist arsenals.

Another major part of the problem lies in the governments that supply arms and explosives to terrorists. They could be stopped only by international agreements, which are unlikely in the present political climate.

Depriving the terrorists of the more advanced weapons of mass destruction is also problematical. Nuclear materials need special protection at every step. Measures already in use in some countries, but urgently needing to be adopted universally, include heavily reinforced and tamper-proof containers for shipment, equally secure vaults for storage, electronic surveillance systems, and well-trained, well-equipped guards. One intriguing protective measure involves the use of a plastic foam that hardens instantaneously, becoming impenetrable. The foam would be sprayed into nuclear storage vaults immediately in case of attack.

These measures apply mainly to safeguarding nuclear weapons. Pilferage of nuclear materials, particularly the widely produced plutonium 239, is more difficult to control. All nuclear installations are expected to keep careful track of every gram of nuclear material. Yet reports persist of unexplained disappearances, sometimes of considerable quantities but more often of small quantities that accumulate over long periods. Unfortunately, this source is more likely to provide terrorists with a realistic basis for nuclear blackmail than the more commonly imagined attempt to steal a complete nuclear weapon.

Control of chemical and biological agents is still more dubious. They are too easily available, or too simple to produce, to come under any feasible regulatory procedures.

The regrettable conclusion is that the prospects for weapons control are not encouraging. The search for workable new approaches nevertheless goes on.

A second category of measures for preventing and deterring terrorism is the improvement of physical security. The task applies both to potential human targets and to endangered installations.

Diplomats, government officials, and high-ranking corporate executives have been the most frequent civilian victims of terrorist action. Security experts recommend that they keep a low profile while abroad, shunning public attention whenever they can. They are also advised to vary their daily travel routes between home and office.

Recent assassination attempts have made increasing use of hand-held anti-tank rockets, along with the more usual automatic weapons, against vehicles carrying major public figures. When such individuals are obligated to proceed in public, as for example in a motorcade during some official ceremony, their vehicles should be armored as well as equipped with bulletproof glass.

The American ambassador to Lebanon was saved from an assassination attempt in 1980 because he was traveling in such a specially reinforced car. Swift action by the armed and trained professional security officers accompanying him also helped thwart the killers.

According to Anthony C. E. Quainton, Director of the U.S. State Department's Office for Combatting Terrorism, American diplomats in training receive elaborate anti-terrorist indoctrination:

> At the Foreign Service Institute in Washington we offer a course on terrorism and coping with violence which . . . [includes] such subjects as surveillance recognition, travel precautions and countering vehicular kidnapping, recognition of and defenses against letter or parcel bombs, residential security [and] hostage survival.

The requirements for protecting vulnerable public buildings and other installations are well known. They include sturdy barriers, rigorous identification procedures at all entry points, and external and internal surveillance both by patrols and by electronic devices. Especially valuable are the recently developed and highly sophisticated intrusion sensors, which are capable of detecting vibrations, sounds, and unusual temperature changes.

A third category of preventive action is intelligence gathering. Its overall aim is accurate and timely prediction; that is, to discover what the terrorists are planning in time to prevent them from carrying out their plans.

Intelligence agents seek first of all to pin down the activists' identities. New techniques have been developed for building up complete individual files. The information these contain can get astonishingly detailed. Besides photographs, fingerprints, and other routine information, the militants' blood types, hair chemistries, medical and dental histories, personal habits and quirks, even their preferences in food, drink, music, and reading are sought out and recorded. Everything that can be learned about their political ideas and past associations will likewise be grist for the mill.

Next come the organizations. Vital information includes their command structures, the size of their membership, their training, armament and equipment, their sources of financial and political support.

Once the facts have been collected, they are fed into computerized information-retrieval systems. Anti-terrorist forces need to have the data available almost instantaneously. It may be needed in the country where it was gathered, or it may be passed on to other countries and international bodies.

International cooperation in this field has taken great strides in recent years. Top government officials from most West European countries have been meeting regularly since 1978 to exchange information and coordinate anti-terrorist strategies. The heads of their police forces are also in regular contact.

Computerized data systems have been set up all across Europe. They contain a vast quantity of information: license-plate numbers, descriptions of suspect automobiles, movements across borders, transfers of illegally obtained funds such as ransom payments, terrorists' personal files. The West German computer system alone contains some ten million items of information.

Anthony Quainton believes that U.S. intelligence has improved greatly over the past decade. "We now do have computer data bases," he declared in September 1980, "which enable us rapidly to factor information about terrorist groups into our crisis management system." The United States has also sharpened its ability to gain advance warning of terrorists' intentions. "Almost every week, somewhere in the world, we are informed of a specific threat against one of our diplomats or embassies, or against a private corporation, airline, or executive." Such information is transmitted to targeted individuals and institutions at once.

The techniques used for acquiring all this information will be familiar to any detective-story buff or James Bond fan. Undercover agents, informers, wire taps, electronic surveillance, stakeouts, tailing suspects, interrogations both subtle and forceful—all these and other methods can be and have been called into play.

This "spy business" has ballooned into a tremendous worldwide industry during the past three decades. Its unprecedented growth, along with some of the unscrupulous methods it all too frequently employs, have caused concern among defenders of human rights. With so much personal information collected and stored in vast computer banks, the individual's right to privacy is endangered in ways that were previously inconceivable.

It is one thing to hunt for terrorists. In too many countries today, that hunt has been expanded to include recording and cataloging and computerizing almost any expression of disagreement with those in power. Citizens hesitate to express open criticism of their government. They fear that their statements may be entered into some secret police dossier somewhere, perhaps to be used against them at some unforeseeable time. Wherever and whenever that happens, the fundamental freedoms of speech, press, association, and peaceful protest are at risk.

There is an old saying: "One man's terrorist is another man's freedom fighter." Citizens of democratic societies have a duty to see to it that "freedom fighters" are not swept up in over-enthusiastic campaigns against terrorists.

Undue harassment of innocent citizens can even hurt the intelligence-gathering process. Useful information needed for anti-terrorist operations is often volunteered by the public. When ordinary citizens begin to suspect that their government is really seeking to eliminate all opposition, not just terrorists, cooperation dries up.

A fourth aspect of the deterrence problem relates to the treatment dealt out to militants when they are caught. They have been released in so many cases that some experts have labeled terrorism "a low-risk occupation for the terrorists." The Israel Information Center conducted a survey in the mid-1970s. Over two hundred Palestinian terrorists had been arrested for violent acts committed outside the Middle East, mostly in Europe, between 1968 and 1975. By the latter date, only three were still in jail.

Political factors come into play to persuade governments not to press these prosecutions. Arab activists have been the most frequent beneficiaries. European governments dependent on Arab sources for oil have sought to avoid offending their suppliers.

Probably the most notorious case is that of Abu Daoud, who masterminded the 1972 Munich massacre of Israeli Olympic athletes. He was captured soon afterward by the French. West Germany, the country where the crime had been committed, was legally obligated to make every effort to bring him to trial. They asked the French to extradite Abu Daoud to Germany. Instead, the French arranged for him to be flown to Algeria, a favorite haven for terrorists. There have been many such cases since then.

The effect of such lenient policies is easy to imagine. Recruitment into terrorist ranks and ever bolder challenges to authority are encouraged. Authoritative public declarations that terrorists will be prosecuted, and if convicted will face certain and severe punishment, can only have a restraining effect. Countries where such policies are known to be in force have suffered less revolutionary violence than those that have been soft on this issue.

The prosecution of terrorists must be conducted with all the safeguards provided by law. Democratic societies cannot sacrifice their citizens' hard-won legal protection for the sake of swift but possibly arbitrary justice.

It is worth remembering that the revolutionaries' strategy is often designed to cause restrictions of individual liberties and tough repressive measures. The response of the West German government to a series of terrorist killings is cited by some legal experts as an example of overreaction. Persons accused of "terrorist conspiracy" can be kept in jail up to five years without trial. The right of habeas corpus does not apply in such cases; that is, the authorities cannot be compelled to release an accused person if they fail to convince a court they have valid reasons for holding him. Defendants' mail can be opened and read by the authorities. Contacts between prisoners and their attorneys have been severely restricted.

One German citizen arrested during a protest demonstration received a sentence of eighteen months on a charge of blocking the road. The experience subsequently drove him to join a terrorist gang. Another, charged with stone-throwing, served six months in jail before coming to trial. He was acquitted—and promptly turned terrorist.

Similar criticisms have been made of the policies enforced by the British in their campaign against the IRA. According to U.S. Senator Jeremiah Denton, chairman of the Senate Subcommittee on Security and Terrorism, these include

> routine detention for up to seven days without preferring charges; coercive interrogations sanctioned by law . . . and, in some cases, trial without jury pursuant to provisions weighted heavily against the accused, including the placing of the burden of proof on the defendant.

"Coercive interrogations" is a tactful expression for torture.

The ultimate punishment—the death sentence for convicted terrorists—is currently being debated in several parts of the world. Besides the reasons usually advanced in its favor, a special reason is often cited in terrorist cases. Many violent actions, often including the seizure of hostages, have been taken solely to secure the release of imprisoned extremists. Execution, it is argued, would eliminate at least this one cause of violence.

Opponents of the death penalty point out that there is no way of knowing whether action is planned for the release of any specific convicted individuals. Executing them would therefore be done on the basis of a mere possibility. The morality of such an act would be difficult to defend.

Terrorists who have caused the death of innocent persons are another matter. They can be punished under the criminal laws that apply to homicide. The death penalty can be and has been invoked in those countries where it is still in effect.

The death penalty has two drawbacks peculiar to terrorism. First, dead terrorists supply revolutionary propagandists with useful martyrs. Their photographs and other personal mementos become objects of veneration, extremely potent for stirring up popular fervor and especially for recruiting the young. The hope that death sentences will deter would-be terrorists must be measured against this complication.

Second, executions often provoke retaliation. Far from being deterred, terrorists have responded with acts of vengeance. The overall level of violence tends to rise rather than fall.

2.   Response to Terrorist Action

Bombings, assassinations, and robberies, on the one hand, usually call for no counteraction other than the hunt for the perpetrators. Kidnappings, hijackings, and hostage-taking, on the other hand, require some sort of reasoned response. Several alternatives are available. When citizens are being held hostage, even if only a single kidnap victim is involved, the authorities face some agonizing decisions. These include the following:

• Should they negotiate with the terrorists?

- What concessions, if any, should they offer in return for the hostages' safe release?
- Will the granting of concessions encourage future attacks?
- At what point, if ever, should they use force in an attempt to rescue the hostages?
- Under what circumstances is a rescue effort worth the risk to the hostages' lives?

Expert opinion is divided between the hard-liners who oppose negotiations, concessions, or ransom payments of any kind and the soft-liners who urge a more flexible approach.

Hard-liners argue that the no-negotiation policy should be made public in advance. It should then be strictly adhered to in practice. Lives will be saved because activists will be unlikely to seize hostages when they have no possibility of gaining anything by it.

The two countries that have adopted the toughest line are Israel and the United States. Israel declared its policy in the early 1970s: it would never negotiate. Since then its response in hostage situations has consistently been to attack with specially trained troops.

These operations have sometimes proven costly. In May 1974, for example, Palestinian raiders seized ninety Israeli teenagers and held them hostage in a school at Ma'alot. The security forces assaulted the place and killed or captured all of the Palestinians, but the terrorists had time to kill twenty youngsters and injure seventy others. In 1975 another Palestinian raid took possession of a hotel in Tel Aviv, with numerous hostages. Again, the Israelis attacked. Eight hostages died in the ensuing shootout.

Nevertheless, the hard-line policy has paid off in that hostage seizures in Israel and aboard its aircraft as well have ceased.

American policy was stated as early as 1973 by President Nixon:

> Once the terrorist has a demand . . . that is satisfied, he then is encouraged to try it again; that is why the position of your government has to be one . . . of not submitting to international blackmail.

President Reagan reaffirmed the American attitude in his welcoming speech to the hostages released by the Iranians in January 1981: "Let terrorists be aware that . . . our policy will be one of swift and effective retribution . . . there are limits to our patience." Secretary of State Alexander Haig reinforced the President's statement that same day. He announced that the policy would apply not only to terrorists but also to those governments that "condone or encourage terrorist acts," as Iran had done.

The no-negotiations policy has been challenged. Its critics point out that U.S. policy has actually been more flexible than these public statements indicate. An example is the 1977 seizure of three Washington, D.C., buildings belonging to a Jewish organization, B'nai Brith, by black members of the Hanafi Muslim sect. They held 134 hostages for about forty hours, abusing some of them quite brutally.

Most of the raiders' demands were rejected, but some were agreed to. A motion picture had recently opened that was offensive to the sect on religious grounds; the authorities got the film removed from theaters at least temporarily. After the Hanafis had surrendered and released all the hostages, their leader was freed on bail.

This concession was denounced by many at the time as excessively soft, but the leader was arrested soon afterward for threatening the lives of several people. Ultimately he and eleven others were convicted; he was sentenced to serve a minimum of forty-one years in prison. The flexible response had worked. With militants so fiercely convinced of the justice of their cause, a tougher attitude might well have endangered the hostages' lives.

Despite President Reagan's tough-sounding words, the Iranian hostage crisis was actually resolved by negotiations. These had been going on for months between the Iranians, intermediaries from various other countries, and U.S. diplomats. The 444-day ordeal of the fifty-two American hostages ended only when the U.S. assented to certain Iranian demands.

Flexibility has also been advocated by the Task Force on Disorders and Terrorism set up by the federal government's Law Enforcement Assistance Administration in the late 1970s. The task force admitted that the hard-line approach might be appropriate under certain circumstances. But it added that "it serves little purpose to announce such a policy in advance, and such an announcement may indeed have an adverse effect."

Other experts point out that concessions are often not the only purpose of hostage seizures. They may not even be the most important one. The real goal in many instances is to focus public attention on a set of grievances, whether real or only alleged. The hostage-takers will often have prepared some sort of inflammatory political statement, which they demand be published or broadcast. Such statements seldom have the slightest effect on the public. They are almost invariably expressed in such ultra-radical jargon that they are incomprehensible to the ordinary citizen. This kind of concession seems a cheap price to pay for the lives of innocent hostages.

Psychological factors can play a crucial role during the tense hours of a hostage crisis. Syracuse University Professor Murray S. Miron notes that the hostage-takers have pledged themselves to a drastic action, killing the hostages, if their demands are not met. In most cases they do not really wish to carry out this threat. They need some powerful excuse to make it appear as if they had yielded to irresistible force. Granting them some token concessions may ease their decision to give up. As Miron puts it, the authorities should "give the person a chance to back down without losing face."

Another specialist in this field, Harvey Schlossberg, a psychiatrist and former New York City detective, declares that negotiation can serve as a form of therapy for the terrorists. It is essential to relieve their anxieties and tensions, to "cool them down," to bring them to a point where they can deal with reality in a rational, nonviolent manner.

Once the decision has been made to negotiate, the process requires highly skilled and experienced experts. Negotiation is a delicate, complex, high-pressure art. Fortunately, top experts are available.

Probably best known are the men and women of the New York City Police Department's Hostage Negotiating Team. Its coordinator is the celebrated Captain

Frank Bolz. He has helped train negotiators for the FBI, many other police forces, and several foreign specialists as well. Bolz works very closely with Schlossberg. The New York team has persuaded hostage-takers to surrender in over one hundred instances. Not a single hostage, terrorist, or police officer has ever been hurt in any of these situations.

Bolz declares that his team will negotiate all but two concessions: it will never agree to provide weapons to the terrorists, and it will never exchange hostages for members of the team. Turning police officers over to the militants transforms the situation into a "family" problem, making unemotional responses difficult.

Negotiation should always be considered as a first option, according to Bolz. One can always escalate to a more violent response, but one can never de-escalate once violent action has begun.

No matter how skilled and patient the negotiators, some situations cannot be resolved peaceably. There comes a time when force is the only viable option. Police or commando troops or other specially trained men must assault the place where the hostages are being held. The terrorists must be disarmed and captured, incapacitated, or killed if necessary, and the hostages must be rescued—unharmed if possible.

The first requirement for a successful rescue operation is reliable information. The rescuers need to know as much as they can about the physical layout of the place, the exact number of terrorists, and their armament. Faulty information can lead to disaster. This is what happened at Munich in 1972, when all the hostages were killed because the German police opened fire in a situation of uncertainty and haste, giving the raiders an opportunity to respond with deadly effect.

The rescuers' own armament should be selected for precise, instantaneous results. Split seconds will be crucial once the assault begins. If, for example, sharpshooters are to be employed, their rifles should be fitted with telescopic sights and if, as happens all too often, the operation has to be conducted at night, infrared devices as well. Laser sights, which project a red or white circle onto the target, are also useful not only as an aid to accuracy but also for their psychological effect. Terrorists seeing themselves hunted down and picked out by this mysterious ray have been known to surrender on the spot.

The British have developed an ingenious weapon, the "flash-and-bang" or "stun" grenade. It causes a fearsome-sounding explosion and a dazzling flash of light, but does no damage beyond temporarily stunning those in its immediate vicinity. Several were used with excellent effect in October 1977 when British and German commandos cooperated in the rescue of a planeload of hostages held by PFLP militants in Mogadishu, Somalia. The weapon worked again in 1982 when Swiss special police stormed the Polish embassy in Berne to free several hostages and capture four terrorists.

The rescuers will have to accept certain limitations that their adversaries can ignore. Automatic weapons may not be appropriate for the authorities, for instance, even though the terrorists will almost certainly be using them. In the chaos and confusion of the assault, bursts from automatic weapons would be harder to control than single shots and could be as dangerous to the hostages as to their captors. Rescuers may also have to avoid high-powered rifles such as the Armalite or the M-16 and high-powered pistols such as the Browning, whose bullets frequently pass through the intended targets and strike others behind them.

Chemical agents can be used only under carefully controlled circumstances. A wide variety exists to choose from: smoke bombs, teargas and nauseating-gas grenades, nerve agents that cause temporary unconsciousness but not permanent harm.

Use of any such weapons must always be decided with due thought to their possible effects on the hostages. No chemical agent acts instantaneously; terrorists will always have at least a few seconds to act against the hostages before the chemical takes effect. Some can be dangerous in unintended ways: they not only spread their contents but also tend to start fires.

Several countries have developed specialized assault-and-rescue forces. The most experienced is probably the British Special Air Service (SAS), which has seen action in many parts of the world over the past three decades. The SAS is a key element in the forces now fighting the IRA.

West Germany has its GSG9 force, France its Gigène, Italy its Leatherheads, Israel its General Intelligence and Reconnaissance Unit. In what must surely be one of the greatest ironies of history, the Israelis helped organize and train the Germans.

The United States started to develop its own unit, the Blue Light force, in 1978. Its first great test came in the unsuccessful 1980 attempt to rescue the hostages in Iran.

A new industry has grown up in the past decade, consisting of private companies that offer anti-terrorist
services. About forty firms currently advertise a wide
range of activities. They will provide anything from relatively routine assistance, such as training guards and
chauffeurs and setting up electronic defense systems, to
negotiating with hostage-takers and conducting full-
scale rescue assaults.

Their clients are large business corporations alarmed
about the enormous ransoms and other concessions that
terrorists have obtained in over 70 percent of the attacks
on business executives and property. Too often, governments have seemed unable to reduce the threat or
have simply failed to take effective action.

The rise of this new enterprise has disturbed some
observers. They see potential dangers in the assumption
of the security functions of the state by private interests.
These private paramilitary forces could eventually become involved in political crises, taking action against
groups deemed hostile to business. Democracy could be
endangered by the growth of armed forces subject to no
public control. They are at present totally unregulated.

3. The Media in the Middle

The role of the media in terrorist crises has become a
subject of heated dispute, with calls for strict government controls countered by pleas invoking the freedom
of the press.

In the words of a 1979 report by a committee of the
U.S. House of Representatives, the media have sometimes been guilty of "grossly sensationalized reporting."

When this occurs, it can "inflame the incident and exaggerate the terrorists' power and influence."

Such irresponsibility has generally been a result of the intense competition among news organizations. In the drive to scoop their rivals, some have yielded to the "temptation to use dramatic film clips, live radio interviews, shocking (but perhaps circulation-building) headlines."

A troubling example happened during the Hanafi Muslim seizure of the B'nai Brith hostages in Washington. A radio reporter somehow managed to reach the raiders' leader by telephone. Speaking live on the air, he asked whether the terrorists had set any deadline, after which they might act against the hostages. They had not actually considered this idea at all and fortunately did not act on it. But by planting the thought in their minds, the radio interviewer might have worsened the danger to the hostages' lives.

The danger became all too real in another case. At a time when a hijacked plane was sitting on the ground with its cargo of terrorists and hostages, a radio reporter told his audience that the pilot was communicating with the security forces over his radio. The hijackers heard this on their radio. They immediately killed the pilot.

In several instances television news organizations have made arrangements for "secret" interviews with terrorists, who were allowed to shield their identities by wearing hoods during the filming. Such treatment heightened the terrorists' importance, presenting them as glamorous and mysterious figures.

There are at least two dangers in this type of publicity. First, it has produced instances of copy-cat terrorism.

Individuals nurturing all sorts of grievances have imitated what they have seen on television or read in the newspapers. The consequences have sometimes been fatal for the victims. Second, there exists a statistical certainty that audiences as large as those that have witnessed live broadcasts of terrorist incidents will include a number of psychopathic and even psychotic individuals. It is impossible to know exactly how many violent acts have resulted, but the evidence is conclusive that broadcast violence has provoked unstable minds to commit real-life violence.

Such occurrences have produced calls for media censorship. Yet there are serious questions as to the possible effects of downplaying or ignoring terrorist incidents. Unchecked rumors could spread panic among the general public. Terrorists might escalate their violence to a level that could not be ignored in order to compel the public attention they seek.

Terrorist attacks are legitimate news events. The public does have a right to know. The problem lies in establishing proper safeguards so that news stories about such incidents are presented in a rational manner that neither encourages nor exaggerates terrorism.

The media are well aware of the problem and have attempted to respond to it in ways that would make government censorship unnecessary. A 1978 statement by NBC News to a subcommittee of the House Committee on the Judiciary presented a balanced view:

> NBC News has adopted flexible guidelines. . . . We must act with care not to exacerbate any terrorist situation . . . nor to be "used" or manipulated by any of the principals. Our job is to report the essential information without sensationalizing the event.

NBC pledged never to broadcast any terrorist incident live without special permission. Its news people were never to "participate in any way, especially by interviewing kidnappers or hostages during the incident," without first consulting the authorities.

> Because ours is a democratic society, we live by the premise that the benefits of freedom of speech should outweigh the risks of disclosure. Indeed, coverage of a terrorist incident might plant an idea in someone's head to imitate those acts. . . . However, a news organization must balance the public's right to know against that risk.

CBS News stated to the subcommittee that, "In such volatile situations, responsibility must be exercised by news organizations so that the danger to human life inherent in terrorist incidents" is not heightened. CBS contended that

> governmental efforts to suppress newsworthy information raise the most serious constitutional questions. . . . We believe that the public is best served by full and factual reporting of terrorist incidents.

At the same time, CBS reported that it had adopted guidelines regulating its coverage. Virtually all American news organizations have done so within the past few years.

4. The International Response

The 1970s were years of intense effort, much of it under American leadership, to obtain international agreement on a variety of anti-terrorist measures. Results have been limited.

An early success came in 1971, with the ratification by the Organization of American States of a treaty aimed at kidnapping and hostage-taking. These forms of terrorist outrage were then rampant in South America, with U.S. diplomats and business executives the most frequent targets. The treaty had a lengthy title: "Convention to Prevent and Punish Acts of Terrorism Taking the Form of Crimes against Persons and Related Extortions That Are of International Significance."

Agreements for the protection of civil aviation have generally been the easiest to obtain. Every country that has an international airline is concerned about skyjacking. In international conferences at The Hague, Montreal, and Tokyo, the United States pushed for three conventions in this field. By mid-1979 over one hundred countries had ratified these agreements.

In July 1978 the United States met with six of its closest allies in Bonn, West Germany. They agreed to take sanctions against countries that gave sanctuary to hijackers or refused to prosecute them or extradite them to other countries wishing to prosecute them. All flights to and from these countries were to be cut off.

The difficulties have been greater at the United Nations. The only major success has been a General Assembly resolution passed in November 1977. It condemned air piracy and called on all governments to tighten airport security and to prosecute or extradite hijackers. Oddly, some of the very nations that have aided hijackers and given them asylum, such as Algeria, Libya, and South Yemen, voted for this resolution.

American-led efforts to secure enactment of broader U.N. resolutions condemning all forms of terrorism have failed on several occasions. They were opposed by the Soviet bloc and the nations of the Third World, which control a majority in the General Assembly. These nations have always insisted that the resolutions be broadened to include the causes as well as terrorism itself. The result has been resolutions bearing such unmanageable titles as "Measures to prevent international terrorism which endangers or takes human lives or jeopardizes fundamental freedoms, and study of the underlying causes of those forms of terrorism and acts of violence which lie in misery, frustration, grievance and despair and which cause some people to sacrifice human lives, including their own, in an attempt to effect radical changes."

One country of the Soviet bloc, Rumania, has taken an independent stand opposing terrorism and calling for strong action against it. The U.N. representative of this communist country expressed his government's view in forceful terms that must have infuriated radical extremists around the world:

> Acts of terrorism against innocent persons cannot be considered as revolutionary means of struggle even if they are undertaken in the name of a noble cause. . . . We should not confuse or identify the struggle of national liberation of the peoples with terrorism.

Even if they could be arranged, international treaties and U.N. resolutions calling for tough action against terrorism in all its forms would be of limited value. Without a firm will to act, official signatures on formal documents mean little.

The United States learned this to its sorrow during

the 1979–81 detention of its hostages by the Iranians. Resolutions condemning the seizure were passed at the U.N., but only a few close allies joined the United States in actual sanctions against Iran. Yet all responsible governments are supposedly committed to the protection of diplomats in foreign countries and to upholding international law.

The worldwide scourge of terrorism could be eliminated swiftly and permanently if the nations of the world would stand together against it. Until that happens, each country will have to find effective ways to defend itself, perhaps in cooperation with a few loyal friends.

SUGGESTIONS FOR FURTHER READING

1. Books

Alexander, Yonah, David Carlton, and Paul Wilkinson, eds. *Terrorism: Theory and Practice.* Boulder, Colo.: Westview, 1979. A well-chosen collection of scholarly essays.

Becker, Jillian. *Hitler's Children: The Story of the Baader-Meinhof Gang.* New York: Lippincott, 1977. The exciting story of the terrorists who nearly reduced West Germany to chaos in the 1970s.

Begin, Menachem. *The Revolt.* New York: Schumer, 1951. A book by a former terrorist leader that has influenced many more recent extremists. Begin eventually became prime minister of Israel.

Bell, J. Bowyer. *Terror Out of Zion: The Irgun, Lehi, Stern, and the Palestine Underground.* New York: St. Martin's, 1977. A thoughtful portrayal of the Jewish terrorist movements and their controversial role in the creation of the state of Israel.

―――. *A Time of Terror: How Democratic Societies Respond to Revolutionary Violence.* New York: Basic Books, 1978. Traces the development of terrorism since the late 1960s, concluding with recommendations for a balanced response.

Beres, Louis R. *Terrorism and Global Security: The Nuclear Threat.* Boulder, Colo.: Westview, 1979. An exploration of the possibilities of nuclear terrorism, with suggestions for preventive measures.

Clutterbuck, Richard L. *Guerrillas and Terrorists.* Athens: Ohio

188 THE NEW TERRORISM

University Press, 1980. A brief paperback that offers original ideas on the nature and origins of both guerrilla warfare and terrorism.

Demaris, Ovid. *Brothers in Blood: The International Terrorist Network*. New York: Scribner's, 1977. Lengthy but readable. The book's five chapters deal with Carlos, the Palestinians, the Baader-Meinhof Gang, the IRA, and the nuclear threat.

Dobson, Christopher, and Ronald Payne. *The Terrorists: Their Weapons, Leaders, and Tactics*. New York: Facts on File, 1979. A fairly brief survey written in a lively style. Color photographs of many terrorist weapons.

Elliott, J. D., and Leslie K. Gibson, eds. *Contemporary Terrorism: Selected Readings*. Gaithersburg, Md.: International Association of Chiefs of Police, 1978. Particularly useful is the article by Russell and Miller, "Profile of a Terrorist."

Friedlander, Robert A. *Terrorism: Documents of International and Local Control*. Dobbs Ferry, N.Y.: Oceana, 1979–81. A massive three-volume compilation, useful for the study of efforts to achieve international agreements.

Goode, Stephen. *Guerrilla Warfare and Terrorism*. New York: Franklin Watts, 1977. Written for teenage readers. A good basis for comparing the two styles of revolutionary conflict.

Hacker, Frederick J. *Crusaders, Criminals, Crazies: Terror and Terrorism in Our Time*. New York: Norton, 1976. The psychological aspects of terrorism as viewed by a prominent psychiatrist.

Hearst, Patricia C., with Alvin Moscow. *Every Secret Thing*. New York: Doubleday, 1982. The young heiress who was kidnapped and abused by terrorists, yet eventually participated in their operations, tells her story.

Jenkins, Brian. *Embassies under Siege: A Review of U.S. Embassy Takeovers, 1971–1980*. Stanford, Calif.: Rand Corporation, January 1981.

————. *International Terrorism: Trends and Potentialities.* Stanford, Calif.: Rand Corporation, May 1978.

————. *Terrorism in the U.S.* Stanford, Calif.: Rand Corporation, May 1980. Jenkins is one of the world's most respected authorities in this field.

Kupperman, Robert, and Darrell Trent. *Terrorism: Threat, Reality, Response.* Stanford, Calif.: Hoover Institution Press, 1979. The first half is a discussion by the authors. The second is a well-selected group of essays by recognized specialists.

Laqueur, Walter. *The Terrorism Reader: An Historical Anthology.* New York: New American Library, 1978. An indispensable paperback collection of historical source materials.

————. *Terrorism: A Study of National and International Political Violence.* Boston: Little, Brown, 1977. A compact analysis by the internationally esteemed head of the Center for Strategic and International Studies at Georgetown University.

Lineberry, William P., ed. *The Struggle against Terrorism.* New York: Wilson, 1977. Another useful collection.

Liston, Robert A. *Terrorism.* New York: Elsevier-Nelson, 1977. An easy-to-read book designed for youngsters from seventh grade up.

O'Ballance, Edgar. *Terror in Ireland: The Heritage of Hate.* San Francisco: Presidio Press, 1981. The stormy and tragic history of Irish terrorism, vividly presented.

Parry, Albert. *Terrorism: From Robespierre to Arafat.* New York: Vanguard, 1976. A comprehensive history.

Smith, Colin. *Carlos: Portrait of a Terrorist.* New York: Holt, Rinehart & Winston, 1976. A study of the most publicized celebrity among terrorists.

Sterling, Claire. *The Terror Network: The Secret War of International Terrorism.* New York: Holt, Rinehart & Winston, 1981. A penetrating analysis of the sources of terrorist funding, armaments, training, and political backing.

Watson, Francis M. *Political Terrorism: The Threat and the Response*. Washington, D.C.: Robert B. Luce, 1976. Fairly brief but enlightening survey.

2. Periodicals

The already enormous number of articles about terrorism published in periodicals is constantly growing. This brief listing is intended only as a sampling. The titles are self-explanatory in most cases; the others have been briefly annotated.

"As Violence Spreads, Is U.S. Next?" *U.S. News & World Report*, Sept. 14, 1981. Interview with Brian Jenkins.

Beres, Louis R. "Terrorism and the Nuclear Threat." *Current History*, Jan. 1976.

Bishop, Joseph W., Jr. "Can Democracy Defend Itself against Terrorism?" *Commentary*, May 1978. Favors tough policies.

Brzezinski, Zbigniew. "The Failed Mission: The Inside Story of the Attempt to Free the Hostages in Iran." *New York Times Magazine*, April 18, 1982.

Collins, Larry. "Combating Nuclear Terror." *New York Times Magazine*, Dec. 14, 1980. Suggestions by the coauthor of a best-selling novel on this subject.

Franks, Lucinda. "The Seeds of Terror." *New York Times Magazine*, Nov. 22, 1981. An in-depth study of the Weather Underground.

Harden, Blaine. "Terrorism." *Washington Post Magazine*, Mar. 15, 1981. A brief analysis of its various forms.

Jahr, Cliff. "Patty Hearst: Still Living with Fear." *Ladies' Home Journal*, Mar. 1982.

Marshall, Jonathan. "The Business of Terrorism." *Dial*, Jan. 1982. Brief study of an often overlooked aspect.

Rice, Berkeley. "Between the Lines of Threatening Messages." *Psychology Today*, Sept. 1981. The psychological factors underlying extortion threats.

3. U.S. Government Documents

Law Enforcement Assistance Administration, National Advisory Committee on Criminal Justice Standards and Goals. *Disorders and Terrorism: Report of the Task Force on Disorders and Terrorism*. Washington, D.C.: Government Printing Office, 1976.

National Foreign Assessment Center, Central Intelligence Agency. *Patterns of International Terror, 1980*. Washington, D.C.: Government Printing Office, 1981. Fact-filled, but controversial.

Quainton, Anthony C. E. "The Challenge of Terrorism: The 1980s." Washington, D.C.: U.S. State Department, Bureau of Public Affairs, 1980. Quainton was director of the department's Office for Combatting Terrorism.

U.S. House of Representatives, Committee on the Judiciary, Subcommittee on Constitutional and Civil Rights. *Federal Capabilities in Crisis Management and Terrorism*. Washington, D.C.: Government Printing Office, 1979. Discusses possible impact of anti-terrorist legislation on freedom of the press.

———. *Report on Domestic and International Terrorism*. Washington, D.C.: Government Printing Office, 1981. A congressional delegation reports on a visit to Germany and Italy.

INDEX

About the Author

Jonathan Harris earned his BA at the College of the City of New York, his master's degree at Harvard University, his PhD in history at New York University, and his graduate diploma in international relations at the University of Paris, France.

He has taught at NYU, has guest lectured at C. W. Post College and at Adelphi University, and is in his twenty-first year as a social studies teacher at a high school on the North Shore of Long Island.

Dr. Harris has previously published two books, *Hiroshima: A Study in Science, Politics and the Ethics of War* and *Scientists in the Shaping of America*.

ECIA Chapter 2